CONVERSATIONAL HEBREW QUICK AND EASY SERIES

The Most Innovative Technique to Learn the Hebrew Language

PART - 1, PART – 2, PART - 3

YATIR NITZANY

Check out my website:
www.Conversational-Languages.com

Dedication
To all those who ever struggled with learning a foreign language and to Wolfgang Karfunkel

Copyright © 2022
Yatir Nitzany
All rights reserved.
ISBN-13: 978-1951244620
Printed in the United States of America

Foreword
About Myself

For many years I struggled to learn Spanish, and I still knew no more than about twenty words. Consequently, I was extremely frustrated. One day I stumbled upon this method as I was playing around with word combinations. Suddenly, I came to the realization that every language has a certain core group of words that are most commonly used and, simply by learning them, one could gain the ability to engage in quick and easy conversational Spanish.

I discovered which words those were, and I narrowed them down to three hundred and fifty that, once memorized, one could connect and create one's own sentences. The variations were and are *infinite*! By using this incredibly simple technique, I could converse at a proficient level and speak Spanish. Within a week, I astonished my Spanish-speaking friends with my newfound ability. The next semester I registered at my university for a Spanish language course, and I applied the same principles I had learned in that class (grammar, additional vocabulary, future and past tense, etc.) to those three hundred and fifty words I already had memorized, and immediately I felt as if I had grown wings and learned how to fly.

At the end of the semester, we took a class trip to San José, Costa Rica. I was like a fish in water, while the rest of my classmates were floundering and still struggling to converse. Throughout the following months, I again applied the same principle to other languages—French, Hebrew, Italian, and Arabic, all of which I now speak proficiently, thanks to this very simple technique.

This method is by far the fastest way to master quick and easy conversational language skills. There is no other technique that compares to my concept. It is effective, it worked for me, and it will work for you. Be consistent with my program, and you too will succeed the way I and many, many others have.

CONTENTS

The Hebrew Language 7
Reading and Pronunciation in the Hebrew Language 8
Basic Grammatical Requirements of the Hebrew Language 9

Hebrew – I 11
The Program 12
Building Bridges 50
Verb Conjugation 52
Other Useful Tools in the Hebrew Language 61

Hebrew – II 64
Introduction to the Program 65
Travel 67
Transportation 73
City 77
Entertainment 84
Foods 88
Vegetables 94
Fruits 98
Shopping 101
Family 107
Human Body 111
Health 115
Emergencies and Natural Disasters 121
Home 126

5

Hebrew – III 133

Introduction to the Program 134
Office 136
School 142
Profession 148
Business 152
Sports 158
Outdoor Activities 162
Electrical Devices 166
Tools 170
Auto 172
Nature 175
Animals 181
Religion, Holidays, and Traditions 189
Wedding and Relationship 195
Politics 198
Military 204

Congratulations, Now You Are On Your Own 211
Note from the Author 213
Also by Yatir Nitzany 214

The Hebrew Language

The two most ancient written cultures in the world (other than Egyptian with its hieroglyphics) are Chinese in the Far East and Hebrew in the Middle East. Abraham, the father of the three monotheistic faiths, was the first person to speak Hebrew, and the book to introduce his story is the Bible. This awesome literary work covers thousands of years of history, and the book is translated into 126 languages. Hebrew further developed from generation to generation, and its vocabulary became more extensive.

For three millenniums, great works of Hebrew scholars were written in Hebrew and translated into many languages; works such as the Mishna, Talmud, Haggadah, and Derash.

Great philosophers, such as Saadia Gaon (around 800 C.E.) and Rabbi Moses Ben Maimon—known as Maimonides—in the twelfth century, also wrote their philosophies in Hebrew and Arabic (the lingua franca of this historical period). Their works were then translated into Latin and many other languages.

In the medieval era, there were well-known scholars, poets, and authors in Spain, such as Yehuda Halevy, Iben Ezra, Iben Gavirol, and a large number of other writers who expressed themselves in Hebrew.

The Torah, known as the Five Books of Moses in the Bible, was translated into a more comprehensive Hebrew with commentaries by Rashi (a famous rabbi). His native language was French.

In the Enlightenment era, since the great Jewish philosopher Moses Mendelssohn, as well the national poet of Israel, Hayim Nechman Bialik, who expressed himself in the most eloquent Hebrew, creating and adopting it into a modern language and creating new words. Ben Yehuda, who wrote the modern Hebrew dictionary, together with hundreds of writers and superb poets, such as Shaul Tchernichovsky, left an exquisite legacy of literary works in Hebrew. Yet for none of them, Hebrew was their mother tongue. At that time, the language was considered a dead language.

In 1969, Shay Agnon was awarded the Nobel Prize in literature. He wrote in Hebrew, and most of his books are translated into many other languages.

In America, from the Pilgrims' times until 1929, no student was accepted into any Ivy League University, such as Harvard or Yale, unless they read and wrote Hebrew. Most Ivy League universities in the US have a Hebrew Department for Biblical history and the literature of Hebrew scripts.

Nowadays, even at the Universities of Tokyo in Japan and Seoul in South Korea, there are Hebrew departments where Hebrew is taught.

In Israel, where the Hebrew language is the national language, there is the Academy of the Hebrew Language, which assists new learners of the language anytime.

Reading and Pronunciation

*For Middle Eastern languages, including Hebrew, Arabic, Farsi, Pashto, Urdu, Hindi, etc., and also German, to properly pronounce the *kh* or *ch* is essential, for example, *Chanukah* (a Jewish holiday) or *Khaled* (a Muslim name) or *Nacht*("night" in German). The best way to describe *kh* or *ch* is to say "ka" or "ha" while at the same time putting your tongue at the back of your throat and blowing air. It's pronounced similarly to the sound that you make while clearing your throat of phlegm.

*In Hebrew, the accent *aayin* is pronounced as 'aa, and is pronounced deep at the back of your throat, rather similar to the sound one would make when gagging. In the program, the symbol for *ayin* is '*aa* or '*oo*.

**Ha* is pronounced as "ha." Pronunciation takes place deep at the back of your throat, and for correct pronunciation one must constrict the back of the throat and exhale air while simultaneously saying "ha." In the program, this strong *h* ("ha") is emphasized whenever *ah, ha, eh, he,* and *oh* is encountered.

Please keep all these in mind whenever you come across any of these accents in the program.

Basic Grammatical Requirements of the Hebrew Language

*In the Hebrew language, adjectives come after the noun, for example, "sunglasses" - משקפיים / *Mishkafaei* - משקפי ("glasses")*Shemesh* - שמש ("sun"). The same rule also applies for possessive adjectives. For example, "your" / *shelcha* / שלך; "my" / *sheli* / שלי; and "his" or "hers" / *sehlo* - שלו or *shela*- שלה, etc., will always follow the noun, and the article "the" / *ha* / ה... will always precede the noun. For example:

* "your office" / *Ha*- ה ("the") *misrad* - משרד ("office") *shelcha* - שלך("your")

* "his house" / *Ha* - ה ("the") *ba-it* - בית("house") *shelo* - שלו ("his")

* "my place" / *Ha* - ה ("the") *makom* - מקום ("place") *sheli* - שלי("my")

*The word *et* - את in the Hebrew language is a term which is used in order to indicate a definite or direct object, but it depends on how it is used in a sentence. *Et* doesn't directly translate into the English language. So to say "I read," you would say, *Ani Koreh* - אני קורא. To say "I read the book," you wouldsay, *Ani Koreh et ha'sefer* - אני קורא את הספר. Because *sefer* - ספר ("book") is definite and the direct object, you need both the *et* and the *ha*-. *Et* doesn't have to be followed by a "the" suffix *ha*- ("the") when it is definite without the *ha*-. Such cases include names, so *Ani Koreh Et Shakespeare* - אני קורא את שייקספיר would be "I read Shakespeare." *Et* is also very commonly used when describing "that," for example, "I want that" would be *ani rotze et ze* - אני רוצה את זה. Just keep in mind that *et* is actually a preposition wthat is placed before any definite direct object.

*In Hebrew, "because" / *biglal* - בגלל is always followed by "that" / *shae* - ש.... For example, "because I go" is *biglal shae ani olech* - בגלל שאני הולך.

*In Hebrew, the article *"a"* doesn't exist. For example, in the English language "a book" in Hebrew would translate to *sefer* - ספר. Another example is "I want to buy a house" / *ani* ("I") - אני *rotze* ("want") - רוצה *liknot* ("to buy") - לקנות *beit* ("house")- בית.

*In the English language, first person verbs usually begin with "I am" and end with -ing. However, in Hebrew there is no -ing, and there is no "am." There is just "I," ani - אני. So "I am going" is "*Ani olech*" - אני הולך.

*Also, in Hebrew, "you're" is *ata* - אתה. There is no "are"; there is only "you," *ata*. Though there is "are you," *ha'iim ata* - האם אתה.

*In Hebrew grammar, gender is always used. In Hebrew, every noun is either masculine or feminine and sometimes both. In this program, whenever you encounter (m.), it will signify "masculine," and (f.) will signify "feminine."

*In Hebrew, in relation to compound words, the article precedes the second word. "Where is **the** train station?" / *eifo tachanat **ha**rakevet?* / איפה התחנת רכבת?

*In Hebrew regarding a statement with the definite article of a noun, the article precedes the adjective as well.
For example:
"where is **the** public transportation?" / *eifo **ha** tachbura **ha** tziburit?* / איפה התחנה הציבורית?

*In hebrew to signify "and" we use *ve* - ו... or *oo* - או. Any word beginning with *b, v, m, p,* or *f* prior to them *ve* - ו.. / "and" will become *oo* - או...
*Gan **oo** vait* / "garden **and** house" / גן ובית
*Yerakot **oo** feirot* / "vegetables **and** fruits" / ירקות ופירות

Conversational Hebrew Quick and Easy
The Most Innovative Technique to Learn the Hebrew Language

Part I

YATIR NITZANY

Translated by:
Semadar Mercedes Friedman

The Program

I / I am – Ani - אני
With you - (male) Itch'a - אִתְּךָ
With you - (female) It'ach - אִתָּךְ
With us – Itanu - איתנו
With – Eem - עם
For you - (m) Bishvilcha - בשבילך
For you - (f) bishvilech - בשבילך
You, you are - (M) Atta - אתה
You, you are - (M) (F) ah'tt - את
Are you - (m) Ha'iim atta – האם אתה
Are you - (f) Ha'iim ah'tt – האם את
From – Me – מ...

Sentences composed from the vocabulary you just learned"

Are you from Israel?
(Male) Ha'iim ata/ (female) a'tt mi isra'el?
האם אתה\את מישראל?

I am from Jerusalem.
Ani mi yerushalaym.
אני מירושלים.

I am with you.
(M)Ani it'cha/ (F)it'ach.
אני איתך\איתך.

This is for you.
(m)Zeh bishvilcha/ (f)bishvilech.
זה בשבילך\בשבילך .

*In Hebrew, "are you" is *ha'iim atta* - / *ah'tt* – את \ האם אתה. However, when using "is" or "are" as the present plural form of the verb "to be," such as "you are" / *atta, ah'tt* – את, אתה; "he/she is" / *hu, hee* – הוא, היא; "they are" / *hem, hen* – הם, הן, the "is/are" is omitted from the pronoun or noun. * "He is at home" / *hu beh bayit* – הוא בבית, "the boys are here" / *ha yeladim poe* – הילדים פה.

With him - It-o - איתו
With her - It-a - איתה
This (or) this is - (M) Zeh - זה
This (or) this is - (F)zot - זאת
Without him – Biladav - בלעדיו
Without them - (m) Bila'day'hem - בלעדיהם
Without them - (f)bila'day'hen - בלעדיהן
Always – Tamid - תמיד
At the (or) In - (Male) Beh – ב...
At the (or) In - (Female) ba – בה...
Sometimes – Lefamim - לפעמים
Maybe - Oo'lai - אולי
Maybe - itachen - היתכן
Today – Hayom - היום
He (or) he is – Hu - הוא
She (or) she is – Hee - היא

Are you at the house?
Ha'eem ata ba ba'iit?
האם אתה בבית?

I am always with her.
Ani tamid ita.
אני תמיד איתה.

Are you alone today?
Ha'eem ata levad hayom?
האם אתה לבד היום?

Sometimes I go without him.
Lifa'ameem ani olech biladav.
לפעמים אני הולך בלעדיו.

Was - Haya היה
I was - Ani hayiti - הייתי
To be - Li-hiyote - להיות
Good – Tov - טוב
Here – Poe - פה
Here - Kan - כאן
Here - Hena - הנה
Very - Mei'od - מאוד
And – Ve – ו...
Between – Ben - בין
If – Eim - אם
Now - Ka'et / Achshav – עכשיו \ כעת
Tomorrow – Machar - מחר

I was here with them.
Ani hayiti poe itam.
אני הייתי פה איתם.

You and I.
Ata/ah'tt ve ani.
אתה\את ואני.

I was home at 5pm.
Ha'yti ba ba'eet bei sha'a chamesh achar atzorhaim.
הייתי בבית בשעה חמש אחר הצהריים.

Between now and tomorrow.
Bein achshav lemachar.
בין עכשיו למחר.

This is for us.
Ze bishvileinoo.
זה בשבילנו.

*In Hebrew, when the subject of the sentence is definite, then any nouns, adjectives, or determiners must have *ha* – ה...placed before them. The only exceptions are relative clauses and prepositions, for example, "your son" / *ha'ben shelach* – הבן שלך and "the boy is in school" *ha'yeled beh beit ha'sefer* – הילד בבית הספר.

The – Ha – ה...
A (article) - No equivalent
Same - Oto ha'davar אותו הדבר
Later - Achar-kach אחר כך
Later - yoter meuchar יותר מאוחר
Yes – Ken - כן
Happy - Sam'eiach - שמח
To – Li – ל...
Better - Yoter-tov יותר טוב
preferable - Adif עדיף
Then – Az - אז
Also / too / as well – Gam גם
Also / too / as well – Gam kan גם כן
Very - Mei'od - מאוד

It's better to be home later.
Yoter tov leeh'yot ba ba'yeet mehochar yoter.
יותר טוב להיות בבית מאוחר יותר

If this is good, then I am happy.
Eem ze tov, az ani sam'ei'ach.
אם זה טוב, אז אני שמח.

Yes, you are very good.
(Male) Ken, ata tov mei'od.
כן, אתה טוב מאוד.

Yes, you are very good.
(Female) Ken, att tova mei'od.
כן, את טובה מאוד.

The same day.
Oto ha-yom.
אותו היום.

   *This *isn't* a phrase book! The purpose of this book is *solely* to provide you with the tools to create *your own* sentences!

Ok – Beseder - בסדר
Even if - Afilu im אפילו אם / **Even if** - Lamrot – למרות
Afterwards – Acharei אחרי
Afterwards – Achar kach – אחר כך
After – Acharei - אחרי
Worse - Garo'aa - גרוע
Where - Eifo איפה
Where - Heychan - היכן
Everything - ha'kol הכל / **Anything** - Kol davar כל דבר
Somewhere - Eifo shh 'hu איפשהו
Somewhere - Hey chan shh 'hu – היכנשהו
What – Ma - מה
Almost – Kimaat - כמעט
There – Sham - שם

Afterwards is worse.
Acharkach zeh yoter garo'aa.
אחר כך זה יותר גרוע.

Even if I go now.
(m)Afilu im ani holech/(f)holechet achshav.
אפילו אם אני הולך\הולכת עכשיו.

Where is everything?
Heychan kol-davar?
היכן כל דבר?

Maybe somewhere.
Oolai heychan shh'hu.
אולי היכנשהו.

What? I am almost there.
Mah? Ani kimat sham.
מה? אני כמעט שם.

Where are you?
Eifo ata/ah'tt?
איפה אתה\את?

Good morning - Boker tov – בוקר טוב
How are you - (m) Ma'shlomcha - מה שלומך
How are you - (f) Ma'shlomech- מה שלומך
Without us - Bila'dei'nu - בלעדינו
Hello – Shalom - שלום
What is your name - (m) Ma shimcha - מה שמך
What is your name - (f) Ma shmech - מה שמך
How old are you - (m) Ben kama ata- בן כמה אתה
How old are you - (f) Bat kama ah'tt – בת כמה את
Already – Kvar - כבר
Son - Ben בן
Daughter - Baat – בת
Still - Ad'aain - עדיין
House - Ba'itt - בית
Car – Mechoniit - מכונית

Good morning, how are you today?
Boker tov, ma'shlomcha/ma'shlomech hayom?
בוקר טוב, מה שלומך \ מה שלומך היום?

Hello, what is your name?
Shalom, ma shimcha/shmech?
שלום, מה שמך\מה שמך?

How old are you?
Ben kama ata/bat kama ah'tt?
בן כמה אתה\בת כמה את?

Where are you from?
Mi eifo ata/att?
מאיפה אתה\את?

She is not in the car, so maybe she is still at the house?
Hee lo ba mechoniit, az oo'lai hee ad'aain ba-ba'itt?
היא לא במכונית, אז אולי היא עדיין בבית?

I am in the car already with your son and daughter.
Ani kvar ba mechoniit eim ha ben ve ha baat shelach.
אני כבר במכונית עם הבן והבת שלך.

Thank you – Todah - תודה
For – Bishvil - בשביל
That (or) **that is** - (m) Zeh זה
That (or) **that is** - (f) Zot – זאת
It is – Zeh - זה
Time – Zman - זמן
No / not – Lo - לא
Late – Meuchar - מאוחר
Away - (m)Rachok רחוק
Away - (f)rechoka – רחוקה
Similar – Domeh - דומה
To go – Llalechet - ללכת
Almost - Kim'aat - כמעט

Thank you, Yossi.
Toda lecha Yossi.
תודה לך יוסי.

It is almost time to go.
Zeh kimat ha z'man lalechet.
זה כמעט הזמן ללכת.

I am not here, I am away.
Ani lo poe, ani rachok/rechoka.
אני לא פה, אני רחוק\רחוקה.

That house is similar to ours.
Ha ba'iit hazei dom'ae leshelanu.
הבית הזה דומה לשלנו.

*In Hebrew, there are three ways of describing time:
Zman - זמן / "era": "this isn't the right time" / *ze lo ha-zman ha'mat'him* – זה לא הזמן המתאים
Pa'am (singular) - פעם / *pa'mim* - פעמים (plural): "first time" / *pa'am harishona* – פעם הראשונה or "three times" / *shalosh pa'amim* – שלוש פעמים.
Sha'ha - שעה / "hour": "What time is it?" / *Ma ha'sha'ha?* - ?מה השעה

Other - Acher אחר
Other - Shonei שונה
Side – Tzad - צד
Until – Ad - עד
Yesterday – Etmol - אתמול
Without - Bl'ee בלי
Without - Le'lo ללא
Since – Meaz - מאז
Day – Yom - יום
Before – Lifnei - לפני
But - Aval אבל
Hard – Kasheh - קשה
Impossible - Bilti'efshari – בלתי אפשרי
However - Oolam – אולם

I am from the other side.
Ani mae hatsad ha shainee.
אני מהצד השני.

But I was here until late yesterday.
Aval ani ha'yitti poe aa'd meuchar etmol.
אבל אני הייתי פה עד מאוחר אתמול.

The coffee is without sugar.
Ha'kafei bl'ee sucar.
הקפה בלי סוכר.

This is very hard, but it's not impossible.
Zeh mei'od kasheh, aval ze lo bilti'efshari
זה מאוד קשה, אבל זה לא בלתי אפשרי.

*This *isn't* a phrase book! The purpose of this book is *solely* to provide you with the tools to create *your own* sentences!

I say / I am saying - (m)Ani omer - אני אומר
I say / I am saying - (f)Ani omeret - אני אומרת
I want - (m)Ani rotzeh - אני רוֹצָה
I want - (f)Ani rotza – אני רוֹצָה
I go / I am going - (m)Ani holech - אני הולך
I go / I am going - (f)Ani holechet – אני הולכת
I need - (m)Ani tza'rich - אני צריך
I need - (f)Ani tz'rei'cha – אני צריכה
I see / I am seeing - (M)Ani ro'eh - אני רוֹאֶה
I see / I am seeing - (F)Ani ro'ha - אני רוֹאָה
To see - Li-rote - לראות
Everywhere - Bechol makom – בכל מקום
My – Sheli - שלי

I am saying no!
Ani omer/omeret lo!
אני אומר\אומרת לא!

You need to be at home.
Ata tzarich leeh'yot ba ba'yeet.
אתה צריך להיות בבית.

I see light outside.
Ani ro'eh/ro'ha orr bachutz.
אני רוֹאֶה\רוֹאָה אור בחוץ.

What time is it right now?
Ma ha'sha'ha achshav?
מה השעה עכשיו?

I see this everywhere.
Ani ro'eh/ro'ha et ze bechol makom.
אני רוֹאֶה\רוֹאָה את זה בכל מקום.

*In the English language, first person verbs usually begin with "I am" and end with -*ing*. However, in Hebrew there is no -*ing*, and there is no "am." There is just "I," *ani* - אני. So "I am going" is "*Ani olech –* אני הולך."

Without you - (M)biladecha – בִּלְעָדֶיךָ
Without you - (F)bila'daeich - בִּלְעָדַיִךְ
Cousin - (M) Ben dode – בן דוד
Cousin - (F) bat doda – בת דודה
Happy - (M)Samae'ach - שמח
Cousin - (F)smecha - שמחה
Easy – Kal - קל
Night – Laila - לילה
Light – Orr - אור
Outside - Hachutza החוצה
Outside - bachutz – בחוץ
To – Li – ל...
To sell – Limkor - למכור
That – Sheh – ש...
That he is - (m)sheh hu - שהוא
That she is – (f)sheh he - שהיא

I want to see this in the day.
Ani rotzeh/rotza lir-ote et ze ba yom.
אני רוֹצֶה\רוֹצָה לראות את זה ביום

I am happy to be here without my cousin.
Ani samae'ach/smecha li-hiyot poe b'lee haben-dod sheli.
אני שמח\שמחה להיות פה בלי הבן דוד שלי.

I need to be there at night.
Ani tza'rich/tz'rei'cha li-hiyot sham ba-laila.
אני צריך\צריכה להיות שם בלילה.

Is it easy to sell this table?
Haiim kal limkor et hasholchan ha ze?
האם קל למכור את השולחן הזה?

I need to know that that is a good idea.
Ani tzarich/tzraicha lada'at sheh ze ra'aayon tov.
אני צריך לדעת שזה רעיון טוב.

*In the last sentence, we use "that" as a conjunction *(sheh – ש...)* and a demonstrative pronoun *(ze)*.

Place – Makom - מקום
To find – Limtzo - למצוא
To look - Le-histakel - להסתכל
To look for / to search – Lechapes - לחפש
Near, close - Al yad - ליד
Near, close - karov – קרוב
To use - Le-hishtamesh - להשתמש
To know - La-da'aat - לדעת
To decide - Le-hachlit - להחליט
To wait – Lechakot - לחכות
Book – Sefer - ספר

This place is easy to find.
Kal limtzo et hamakom hazeh.
קל למצוא את המקום הזה.

I am saying to wait until tomorrow.
Ani omer/omeret lechakote aa'd machar.
אני אומר\אומרת לחכות עד מחר.

I want to use this.
Ani rotzeh/rotza le-hishtamesh be zeh.
אני רוֹצֶה\ רוֹצָה להשתמש בזה.

Is it possible to look for this book in the library?
Efshar lechapes et ha sefer ba sifriya?
אפשר לחפש את הספר בספריה?

Is this place near?
Ha'eem ha makom hazei karov?
האם המקום הזה קרוב?

I want to know where is the grocery store.
Ani rotzeh/rotza lada'aat heychan chanut ha-makolet.
אני רוֹצֶה\ רוֹצָה לדעת היכן חנות המכולת.

Because - Mekeivan sheh ש מכיוון...
Because - biglal sheh ש בגלל...
Because - Ki כי
Them / They - (M)Hem - הם
Them / They - (F) Hen - הן
Their - (M)Shela-hem - שלהם
Their - (F)shelahen - שלהן
Mine – Sheli - שלי
To understand – Lehaveen - להבין
Problem - Be'aya בעיה
Problems - Be'ayot בעיות
I can – Ani (m)yachol – אני יכול
I can – Ani (f)yechola – יכולה
Can I? – Ha'iim ani (m) yachol? האם אני יכול?
Can I? – Ha'iim ani (f)yechola? – האם אני יכולה?
I do / I am doing - (m)Ani oseh – אני עוֹשֶׂה
I do / I am doing - (f)Ani Osa – אני עוֹשָׂה

I can work today.
Ani yachol la'avod hayoum.
אני יכול לעבוד היום.

I do what I want.
Ani o'sae ma shae ani rotzei.
אני עושה מה שאני רוצה.

That book is mine.
Ha sefer ha ze sheli.
הספר הזה שלי.

I have to understand the problem.
Ani tza'rich/tz'rei'cha le-haveen et ha be'aya.
אני צריך\צריכה להבין את הבעיה.

*In Hebrew, "because" / *biglal* – בגלל (or) *mekeivan* - מכיוון is always followed by "that" / *shae* – ש.... For example, "because I go" is *biglal shae ani olech* - בגלל שאני הולך (or) *mekeivan shae ani olech* – מכיוון שאני הולך.

Food - Ochel / mazon – מזון \ אוכל
Water – Maiim - מים
Hotel - Malon / Beit-malon – בית מלון \ מלון
View – Nof - נוף
There are/ there is – Yesh - יש
Much, many, a lot – Harbei - הרבה
A little – Ktzat - קצת
Both - Shnay-hem - שניהם
To buy – Liknot - לקנות
Two – Shnaim - שניים
Between – Ben - בן
Both – Shnei - שני

There are many tourists in Israel every summer.
Yesh harbei tayarim be Israel kol ka'itz.
יש הרבה תיירים בישראל כל קיץ.

I like this hotel because it's near the beach.
Ani ohev et ha malon hazei kee hoo nimtza le'yad ha chof.
אני אוהב את המלון הזה כי הוא נמצא ליד החוף.

I want to look at the view.
Ani rotzei leheestakel al ha nof.
אני רוצה להסתכל על הנוף.

I want to buy a water bottle.
Ani rotze/rotza liknot bakbok mayim.
אני רוֹצֶה\רוֹצָה לקנות בקבוק מים.

I see the view of the city from my hotel room.
Ani ro'eh et ha nof shel ha irr mi chadar ha malon sheli.
אני רואה את הנוף של העיר מחדר המלון שלי.

I need to decide between both places.
Ani tza'rich/tz'rei'cha le-hachlit ben shnai ha'mekomot.
אני צריך\צריכה להחליט בן שני מקומות.

I am very happy to know that everything is ok.
Ani mei'od samae'ach la-da'aat shae hakol beseder.
אני מאוד שמח לדעת שהכל בסדר.

Parents – Horim - הורים
Why - Mado'a / Lama – מדוע\למה
To say - Lo-mar - לומר
To work - La-avode - לעבוד
I like / I enjoy - (m)Ani o'hev – אני אוהב
I like / I enjoy - (f)Ani o'hevet – אני אוהבת
Something - Ma'shaehu - משהו
Who – Me - מי
We are - Anachnu אנחנו
Building - Binyan בניין
Doctor - Rofei רופא

We are from Haifa.
Anachnu me chaifa.
אנחנו מחיפה.

Your doctor is in the same building.
Ha rofei shelcha neemtza bei oto binyan.
הרופא שלך נמצא באותו בניין.

I like to be at my house with my parents.
Ani o'hev/o'hevet li-hiyot ba- ba'itt eem ha-horim sheli.
אני אוהב\אוהבת להיות בבית עם ההורים שלי.

Why do I need to say something important?
Madoo'a a'lai lomar mashae'hoo chashoov?
מדוע עליי לומר משהו חשוב?

I am there with him.
Ani sham ee-toe.
אני שם איתו.

I like to work.
Ani o'hev/o'hevet la'avod.
אני אוהב\אוהבת לעבוד.

Who is there?
Me sham?
מי שם?

I will be - Ani he'ye – אני אהיה
Good morning - Boker tov – בוקר טוב
Ready - Moo'chan - מוכנים
Soon / quickly - Bekarov בקרוב
Soon / quickly - Ma'her מהר
Soon / quickly - Bem'hera במהרה
Soon / quickly - behekdem בהקדם
Important – Chashuv - חשוב
Busy - (M)Hasuk - עסוק
Busy - (F)Hasuka - עסוקה
Of – Shel - של
Like this – Kacha - ככה

I am busy, but I will be ready quickly.
Ani hasuk/hasuka, aval ani he'ye muchan/muchana bim'hera.
אני עסוק\עסוקה, אבל אני אהיה מוכן\מכונה במהרה.

I want to know if they are here.
Ani rotzei lada'at eem hem kan.
אני רוצה לדעת אם הם שם.

I can go outside.
Ani yachol latzet hachootza.
אני יכול לצאת החוצה.

There is a taxi outside.
Yesh monit bachutz.
יש מונית בחוץ.

Do it like this!
Tahase'e et ze kach!
תעשה את זה כך!

*This *isn't* a phrase book! The purpose of this book is *solely* to provide you with the tools to create *your own* sentences!

How much, how many – Kama - כמה
To bring - Le-havee - להביא
With me – Iti - איתי
Instead – Bimkom - במקום
Only – Rak - רק
When – Matai - מתי
Were - Ha-yu - היו
Without me - Bi'ladai - בלעדיי
You can – Ata yachol – אתה יכול

Only when you can.
(M)Rak matai shei ata yachol.
רק מתי שאתה יכול.
(F)Rak matai shei ah'tt ye'chola.
רק מתי שאת יכולה.

Go there without me.
Lech lesham bila'da'yee.
לך לשם בלעדיי.

How much money do I need to bring with me?
Kama kesef ani tzarich/tzreicha le-havee ee-tee?
כמה כסף אני צריך\צריכה להביא איתי?

It is already there.
Ze kvar sham.
זה כבר שם.

*With the knowledge you've gained so far, now try to create your own sentences!

Fast - Ma'her - מהר
Slow - Le-at - לאט
Inside – Befnim - בפנים
Cold – Kar - קר
Hot – Cham - חם
To Drive - Linhog - לנהוג
To Drive - Lin-so-ah - לנסוע
To eat - Le-echol - לאכול
Do I – Ani – אני
Do I? – Haeem ani? – האם אני?
Lunch – Aruchat hatzo'horaiim – ארוחת הצהריים

I prefer bread instead of rice.
Ani mahadif lechem bimkom orez.
אני מעדיף לחם על אורז.

I need to drive in the car very fast or very slow.
Ani tza'rich/tz'rei'cha linhog ba-mechoniit mei'od ma'her o mei'od le'at.
אני צריך\צריכה לנהוג במכונית מאוד מהר או מאוד לאט.

It is already there.
Ze kvar sham.
זה כבר שם

This is a good meal.
Zot arucha tova.
זאת ארוחה טובה.

I like to eat a hot meal for my lunch.
Ani o'hev/o'hevet leichol aroocha chama la aroochat hatz'hraym.
אני אוהב\אוהבת לאכול ארוחה חמה לארוחת הצהריים.

The winter is very cold in Israel.
Hachoref kar meihod be'israel
החורף קר מאוד בישראל.

To answer - La-anote - לענות
To fly - La-toos - לטוס
To travel – Letayel - לטייל
To learn – Lilmod - ללמוד
How – Eich - איך
To leave - Le-hasheer - להשאיר
Time - Pa-am - פעם
United States - hartzot habrit ארצות הברית
Hill - Giv'ah גיבעה
Mountain - Haar הר

Since the first time.
Meaz ha pa'am ha-rishona.
מאז הפעם הראשונה.

The children are yours!
Ha yeladim shelcha!
הילדים שלך!

I need to answer many questions.
Ani tza'rich/tz'rei'cha la'anote al harbei shaei'lot.
אני צריך\צריכה לענות על הרבה שאלות

I want to fly to the United States today.
Ani rotzeh/rotza la-toos hayom lei hartzot habrit.
אני רוֹצָה\רוֹצָה לטוס היום לארצות הברית.

Our house is on the hill.
Habait shelanu al hagiv'ah
הבית שלנו על הגבעה

*In Hebrew, to leave (a place) is *la-a-zove* - לעזוב; to leave (an object) is *le'hasheer* - להשאיר.

To swim – Lischot - לשחות
To practice – Lehitamen - להלחם
To play – Lesachek - לשחק
Our – Shelanu - שלנו
How – Eich - איך
Pool – Brecha - בריכה
First - (M) Rishon- ראשון
First - (F) Rishona - ראשונה
Money – Kesef - כסף
Enough - Maspik מספיק

I need to learn how to swim at our pool.
Ani tza'rich/tz'rei'cha lilmod eich lischot ba brecha shelanu.
.אני צריך\צריכה ללמוד איך לשחות בבריכה שלנו

I want to leave my dog at home.
Ani rotzei lahasheer et ha kelev sheli ba ba'yeet.
.אני רוצה להשאיר את הכלב שלי בבית

I want to travel the world.
Ani rotzei letayel ba o'lam.
.אני רוצה לטייל בעולם

I want to learn how to play better tennis.
Ani rotzei lilmod lesachek tennis tov yoter.
.אני רוצה ללמוד לשחק טניס טוב יתר

I don' have enough money.
Ein li maspik kesef.
.אין לי מספיק כסף

That is a very tall mountain.
Ze har gavo'ha meihod.
.זה הר גבוה מאוד

Nobody / anyone - Af echad – אף אחד
Against – Neged - נגד
Us / we / we are - Anach'nu - אנחנו
To visit - Le'vaker – לבקר/
Mom – Ima - אמא
To give - La-tet - לתת/
Just – Rak - רק
You *(indirect object)* **– (m)** Lecha- לְךָ/
You *(indirect object)* **- (f)** Lach - לָךְ *(read footnote below)*
Family – Mishpacha - משפחה
Week – Shavuha - שבוע
Than - Mi מ
Than - Mae'asher מאשר

Something is better than nothing.
Mashaehu ze yoter tov mi kloom.
.משהו זה יותר טוב מכלום

I am against.
Ani neged.
אני נגד

Do you do this everyday?
Ata oseh et ze kol yom?
?אתה עושה את זה כל יום

We go to visit my family each week.
Anachnu holechim/holchot levaker et ha mishpacha sheli kol shavuha.
.אנחנו הולכים\הולכות לבקר את המשפחה שלי כל שבוע

I need to give you something.
Ani tza'rich/tz'rei'cha latet lecha/lach mashehu.
.אני צריך\צריכה לתת לְךָ\לָךְ משהו

Lecha / lach is the indirect object pronoun of the pronoun "you," the person who is actually affected by the action that is being carried out.

Someone - (m)Mi-shehu - מישהו
Someone - (f)mi'she'hee - מישהי
Nothing - Shoom davar – שום דבר
Nothing - Kloom כלום
Each / Every — Kol - כל -
Around — Misaviv - מסביב
To walk - La-lechet - ללכת
To meet — Lifgosh - לפגוש
Towards - Likrat לקראת
Towards - Lei'ever לעבר
Five — Chamesh- חמש
Minute - Daka דקה
Minutes - Dakot – דקות

Do you want to meet someone?
Haiim ata rotzeh/rotza lifgosh mi-shehu?
?האם אתה רוֹצֶה\רוֹצָה לפגוש מישהו

I am here tomorrow as well.
Ani poe gam machar.
אני פה גם מחר.

You need to walk around the school.
Ata tzarich / att tzreicha lalechet misaviv la beit ha sefer.
אתה צריך\את צריכה ללכת מסביב לבית הספר.

From here to there, it's just five minutes.
Mi poe le-sham, ze rak chamesh dakot.
מפה לשם, זה רק חמש דקות.

*In Hebrew, you use *haiim* - האם? whenever asking a question, starting with "do," "does," "are," etc., for example:
  * "do you…?" / *haiim ata / ah'tt?* את \ האם אתה?
  * "does he, she…?" / *haiim hu? / hee?* האם הוא\היא?
  * "does the…?" / *haiim ha?* האם ה...?
  * "are they…?" / *haiim hem?* האם הם?
  * "is it possible…?" / *haiim ze efshari?* האם זה אפשרי?

I have - Yesh li – יש לי
I don't have - Ein li – אין לי
To borrow - Le-hash'ill - להשאיל
To borrow - Lilvot לילוות
To Loan - Le-alvot להלוות
Grandfather – Saba - סבא
To want – Lirtzot - לרצות
To stay - Le-hish-a-er - להישאר
To continue - Le-hamshich - להמשיך
To show - Le-harot - להראות
Way – Derech - דרך
School - Beit sefer בית ספר
Located - Memukam ממוקם
Located - Nimtza נמצא
Mall - Kenyon קניון
On / about – Al - על

Why don't you have the book?
Lama ein lecha/lach et ha-sefer?
?למה אין לךָ\ לָךְ את הספר

I want to borrow this book for my grandfather.
Ani rotze le-hash'ill et ha sefer ha ze bishvil saba sheli.
.אני רוצה להשאיל את הספר הזה בשביל סבא שלי

Can you show me the way to the Western Wall?
Ata yachol laharot li et ha-derech la kotel?
?אתה יכול להראות לי את הדרך לכותל

I want to stay in Tel-Aviv because I have a friend there.
Ani rotzei/rotza le'hisha'er bae tel-aviv kee yesh li sham chaver.
.אני רוֹצֶה\רוֹצָה להשאר בתל אביב כי יש לי שם חבר

The school is located near the mall.
Beit ha-sefer memukam leyad ha-kenyon.
.בית הספר ממוקם ליד הקניון

To look like - Le'hiraot kmo – להראות כמו
To prepare - Le-hit-konen - להתכונן
Like (preposition) – Kmo - כמו
Friend – Chaver - חבר
Man - Ish איש
Man - Gever גבר
Woman - Isha אישה
Woman - Geveret גברת
Breakfast - Aruchat boker – ארוחת בוקר
That's why – Lachen - לכן
To show - Le-harot - להראות
With you - (male) Itch'a - אִתְּךָ
With you - (female) It'ach - אִתָּךְ

Do you want to look like a Matan?
Haiim ata/ah'tt rotze/rotza le'hiraot kmo Matan?
האם אתה\את רוֹצֶה\רוֹצָה להראות כמו מתן?

I want to drive and to continue on this way to my house.
Ani rotze lin-so-ah ve le-hamshich ba-derech hazot la-ba'itt sheli.
אני רוצה לנסוע ולהמשיך בדרך הזאת לבית שלי.

I need to show you how to prepare breakfast.
Ani tza'rich/tz'rei'cha le-harote lecha/lach eich le-hachin aruchat boker.
אני צריך\צריכה להראות לךָ\ לךְ איך להכין ארוחת בוקר.

I don't need the car today.
Ani lo tza'rich/tz'rei'cha et ha-mechoniit ha-yom.
אני לא צריך\צריכה את המכונית היום.

I want to come with you.
Ani rotze/rotza lavo itach/ itcha.
אני רוצה לבוא איתך.

To remember - Li-zkor - לזכור
Your – (m) Shelcha - שלך
Your – (f) Shelach - שלך
Number – Mispar - מספר
Hour - Sha-ah - שעה
Dark - Choshech - חושך
Darkness - Chashecha – חשיכה
Grandmother – Safta - סבתא
More - Yoter - יותר
More - Ode - עוד
To think - Lach-shove - לחשוב
To hear - Li-shmoa - לשמוע
To listen - Le-haziin - להאזין
To listen - Le-akshiiv - להקשיב
Last - (m) Acharon - אחרון
Last - (f) Acharona - אחרונה
To speak / to talk – Ledaber - לדבר
To do - La-a-sote - לעשות
A second - Shnee'ya - שנייה

You need to remember your number.
Atta/ah'tt tza'rich/tz'rei'cha li-zkor et ha-mispar shelcha/shelach.
אתה\את צריך\צריכה לזכור את המספר שֶׁלְךָ\שֶׁלָךְ.

This is the last hour of darkness.
Zot ha-sha-ah ha'acharona shel ha chashecha.
זאת השעה האחרונה של החשיכה.

I can hear my grandmother speaking Hebrew.
Ani yachol/yechola lishmo'a et ha savta sheli medaberet ivrit.
אני יכול\יכולה לשמוע את הסבתא שלי מדברת עברית.

I need to think about this more.
Ani tzarich lachshov a'al ze yoter.
אני צריך לחשוב על זה יותר.

To leave - La-a-zove - לעזוב
Again - Shuv שוב
Again - Ode pa'am – עוד פעם
To take – Lakachat - לקחת
To try – Lenasot - לנסות
To rent - Le-ha-zkir - להשכיר
To rent - Lizchor - לשכור
To ask - Le-vakesh - לבקש
To stop – Lehafsik - להפסיק
To turn off – Lechabot - לכבות
Beach - Chof hayam – חוף הים

I need to rent a house on the beach.
Ani tza'rich/tz'rei'cha le-ha-zkir ba'itt al chof hayam.
אני צריך\צריכה לשכורבית על חוף הים.

I want to take this with me.
Ani rotze/rotza lakachat et ze iti.
אני רוֹצֶה\רוֹצָה לקחת את זה איתי.

We want to stop here.
Anachnu rotzim/rotzot la'aatzor poe.
אנחנו רוצים\רוצות לעצור פה.

I need to turn off the lights early.
Ani tzarich/tzreicha lechabot et ha orot mukdam.
אני צריך\צריכה לכבות את האור מוקדם.

Is this for me?
Haiim ze bishvili?
האם זה בשבילי?

Lehafsik – לפסיק is "to cease," and *lahatzor* – לעצור is "to physically stop," for example, "to stop the car" / *lahatzor et ha'mechoniit* – לעצור את המכונית.

*The definition of *chof hayam* – חוף הים is "beach." But the literal definition is "shore of the sea": *chof* - חוף ("shore") *hayam* - הים("of the sea").

To open - Lifto-ach - לפתוח
A bit, a little, a little bit – Ktzat קצת
A bit, a little, a little bit – Mae'at מעט
Sister – Achot - אחות
Nice to meet you - (m) Naiim lahakir otach נעים להכיר אוֹתָךְ
Nice to meet you - (f) Naiim lahakir otcha נעים להכיר אוֹתָךְ
To buy - Liknot לקנות
Something - Mashae'hu משהו
Something - Davar דבר
Name – Shem - שם
Last name - Shem mishpacha – שם משפחה
Door - De-let - דלת
There isn't/ there aren't – Ein אין
Early – Mukdam - מוקדם

I need to open the door for my sister.
Ani tza'rich/tz'rei'cha liftoach et ha de-let bishvil achot'ee.
.אני צריך\צריכה לפתוח את הדלת בשביל אחותי

I need to buy something.
Ani tza'rich/tz'rei'cha liknot mashaehu.
.אני צריך\צריכה לקנות משהו

I want to meet your brothers.
Ani rotzei lifgosh et ha acheem shelcha.
.אני רוצה לפגוש את האחים שלך

Nice to meet you. What is your name and your last name?
Naiim lehakir otcha/otach. Ma hashem shelcha/shelach ve shem ha mishpacha?
נעים לכיר אוֹתָךְ\אוֹתָךְ. מה השם שֶׁלְּךָ\שֶׁלָּךְ והשם משפחה?

*With the knowledge you've gained so far, now try to create your own sentences!

To live (to exist) - Li-chiyot - לחיות
To live (in a place) - Lagoor - לגור
To return - La-cha-zor - לחזור
To hope – Lekavot - לקוות
Without - B'lee - בלי
Hebrew – Ivrit - עברית
Synagogue - Beit knesset בית כנסת
Sad - (M) Atzov - עצוב
Sad - (F)atzova - עצובה

We can hope for a better future.
Anoo yecholeem lekavot le a'ateed tov yoter.
.אנו יכולים לקוות לעתיד טוב יותר

It is impossible to live without problems.
Yee efshar leechyot blee bae'ayot.
.אי אפשר לחיות בלי בעיות

I want to return to the United States.
Ani rotzei/rotza lachzor lei artzot ha breet.
.אני רוֹצֶה\רוֹצָה לחזור לארצות הברית

Why are you sad right now?
Lama ata/ah'tt atzov/atzova achshav?
?למה אתה\את עצוב\עצובה עכשיו

*In the Hebrew language, pronouns become suffixes to the noun, although it isn't incorrect to say *achot shelcha* – אחות שלך. For example:
* "sister" / *achot* - אחות
* "my sister" / *achot'ee* - אחותי
* "your sister" / *achot'cha* - אחותך
* "her sister" / *achota* - אחותה
* "his sister" / *achoto* - אחותו
* "their sister" / *achotam* - אחותם
* "our sister" / *achotainu* - אחותינו

To happen - Li-krote - לקרות
To order - Le-hazmeen - להזמין
To drink – Lishtote - לשתות
To keep – Lishmor - לשמור
To begin / to start - Le-hatchil - להתחיל
To finish – Ligmor - לגמור
Child -(m) Yeled - ילד
Child (f) Yalda - ילדה
Child (plural-m) Yeladim - ילדים
Child (plural-f) Yeladot - ילדות
Woman – Isha - אישה
Excuse me / sorry – Slicha - סליחה

This needs to happen today.
Zeh tza'rich likrote ha yom.
.זה צריך לקרות היום

My child he is here as well.
Ha yeled sheli gam poe.
.הילד שלי גם פה

I want to order a soup.
Ani rotzei/rotza lehazmeen marak.
.אני רוֹצֶה\רוֹצָה להזמין מרק

We want to start the class soon.
Anoo rotzeem lehatcheel et ha shee'oor baehekdem.
.אנו רוצים להתחיל את השיעור בהקדם

In order to finish at three o'clock this afternoon, I need to finish soon
Kedei lesayem bae shalosh achar ha tzoharaeem, ani tzarich/tzreicha lesayem be'ekdem.
.כדי לסיים בשלוש אחר הצהריים, אני צריך\צריכה לסיים בהקדם

To speak / to talk – Ledaber - לדבר
To help - La-azore - לעזור
To smoke - Le'aashen - לעשן
To love / to like - Le-ehove - לאהוב
How – Eich - איך

I want to learn how to speak Hebrew fluently.
Ani rotzei/rotza lilmod eich ledaber ivrit shotefet.
אני רוֹצֶה\רוֹצָה ללמוד איך לדבר עברית שוטפת.

I don't want to smoke again.
Ani lo rotze/rotza le'aashen shuv.
אני לא רוֹצֶה\רוֹצָה לעשן שוב.

I want to help.
Ani rotze/rotza la'aazor.
אני רוֹצֶה\רוֹצָה לעזור.

I love you.
Ani ohev/ohevet otcha/otach.
אני אוהב\אוהבת אוֹתְךָ\אוֹתָךְ.

I see you.
Ani ro'eh/ro'ha otcha/otach.
אני רוֹאֶה\רוֹאָה אוֹתְךָ\אוֹתָךְ.

I need you.
Ani tzarich/tzraicha otcha/otach.
אני צריך\צריכה אוֹתְךָ\אוֹתָךְ.

Otcha / otach - אוֹתְךָ\אוֹתָךְ is the direct object pronoun of the pronoun "you."

*The definition of "child" is *(M)Yeled* - ילד / *(f)yalda* - ילדה however the plural forms are *(p-m)yeladim* - ילדים / *(p-f)yeladot* - ילדות.

To read – Likro - לקרוא
To write – Lichtov - לכתוב
To teach – Lelamed - ללמד
To close – Lisgor - לסגור
To choose - Livchor - לבחור
To prefer - Le'aadif - להעדיף
To put - La-seem - לשים
Less – Pachot - פחות
Sun – Shemesh - שמש
Month – Chodesh - חודש
Permission - Ri-shote - רשות
Exact - Medu'yak - מָדוּיָק
Airport - Sdei tehufa - שדה תעופה
To sleep - Lishon - לישון

In order to leave you have to ask permission.
Kedei lahazov ata chayav/att chayevet levakesh reshoot.
כדי לעזוב אתה חייב \ את חייבת לבקש רשות.

I want to go to sleep now because I need to wake up early in order to take a taxi to the airport.
Ani tzarich/tzraicha lalechet lishon achshav biglal shae ani tzarich/traicha leitorer mukdam kedei lakachat monit lezdei-hatae'oofa.
אני צריך\צריכה ללכת לישון עכשיו בגלל שאני צריך\תריכה להתעורר מוקדם כדי לקחת מונית לשדה תעופה.

Is it possible to know the exact date of the flight?
Haiim ze efshari lada'aat et ha ta-arich ha meduyak shel ha'tissa?
האם זה אפשרי לדעת את התאריך המדויק של הטיסה?

I need this book to learn how to read and write in Hebrew.
Ani tzarich/tzreicha lilmod eich likro ve lichtov bei/ivrit.
אני צריך\צריכה ללמוד איך לקרוא ולכתוב בעברית.

I want to teach English in Israel.
Ani rotzei/rotza lelamed anglit bei yees'ra'el.
אני רוֹצָה\רוֹצָה ללמד אנגלית בישראל.

To turn on – Lehadlik - להדליק
In order – Kedei - כדי
Date – Taharich - תאריך
Possible – Efshari - אפשרי
Exact – Meduyak - מדויק
I talk / I am talking - (m)Ani Medaber – אני מדבר
I talk / I am talking - (f)Ani Medaberet – אני מדברת

I want to turn on the lights and close the door.
Ani rotzei lahadleek ha orot ve lisgor et ha delet.
אני רוצה להדליק את האורות ולסגור את הדלת.

I need to go outside.
Ani tzarich/tzreicha latzet ha'chutza.
אני צריך\צריכה לצאת החוצה.

Is it possible to know the exact date of the flight?
Haiim ze efshari lada'aat et ha ta-arich ha meduyak shel ha'tissa?
האם זה אפשרי לדעת את התאריך המדויק של הטיסה?

I talk with the boy and with the girl in English.
Ani medaber/medaberet eim ha-yeled ve eim ha-yalda be anglit.
אני מדבר\מדברת עם הילד ועם הילדה באנגלית.

I want to pay less than you.
Ani rotzei leshalem pachot mimcha.
אני רוצה לשלם פחות ממך.

I prefer to put this here.
Ani ma'adeef laseem et zei kan.
אני מעדיף לשים את זה כאן.

*The definition of "than" is *mi* – מ.... (However, when combined with a pronoun, it becomes a prefix). For example:
* "than you" / *mimcha* – ממך.
* "than me" / *mimeni* – ממני.
* "than him" / *mimeno* – ממנו.
* "than her" / *mimena* – ממנה.
* "than us" / *me'itanu* – מאיתנו.

Up – Lemaala - למעלה
Down – Lemata - למטה
Below, under – Mitachat - מתחת
Above - Mae'al מעל
Of course - Behechlet בהחלט
Of course - be'vadai – בוודאי
To follow - La-a-kove - לעקוב
New – Chadash - חדש
To arrive - Le'hag'ee'aa - להגיע
Theater - Te'atron - תאטרון
Welcome - Bruchim habaiim – ברוכים הבאים
Dog - Kelev כלב

Of course I can come to the theater, and I want to sit together with you and your family.
Bevadai sheh ani yachol/ye'chola lehag'ee'aa la-te'atron, ve ani rotze/rotza lashevet beyachad itcha/itach ve im ha mishpacha shelcha.
בוודאי שאני יכול\יכולה להגיע לתאטרון, ואני רוצֶה\רוֹצָה לשבת ביחד איתְךָ\איתָךְ ועם המשפחה שלך

If you look under the table, you can see the new rug.
Eem tistakel mitachat lashoolchan, ata tochal lirot et ha marvad ha chadash.
אם תסתכל מתחת לשולחן, אתה תוכל לראות את מרבד החדש.

I can see the sky from the window.
Ani yachol lirot et ha shamayim me'hachalon.
אני יכול לראות את השמיים מהחלון.

The dog wants to follow me to the store.
Ha kelev rotzei lahakov achar'a'ee la chanoot.
הכלב רוצה לעקוב אחרי לחנות.

*In Hebrew "to call (on the phone)" is *lehitkasher* - להתקשר. However, to call out to someone is *likro* - לקרוא.

To allow - Le-harshot - להרשות
To believe - Leha'amin - להאמין
To promise - Le-havtiach - להבטיח
To recognize – Lehakir - להכיר
People – Anashim - אנשים
Far – Rachok - רחוק
Him - Lo לו / **Her** - La לה
Morning - Boker בוקר
Good night - Laila tov – לילה טוב
Except – Milvad - מלבד
So (as in *then*) – Az - אז
So (as in *so much*) - Kol-kach – כל כך

I need to allow him to go with us.
Ani tzareech laharshot lo la lechet eetan'oo.
אני צריך להרשות לו ללכת איתנו.

I can't recognize him.
Ani lo yachol lahakeer oto.
אני לא יכול להכיר אותו.

Come here quickly.
Bo lekan ma'her.
בוא הנה מהר

I need to believe everything except for this.
Ani tza'rich/tz'rei'cha le'ha'amin le'ha-kol milvad zeh.
אני צריך\צריכה להאמין להכל מלבד זה.

I must promise myself not to forget to say good night to my parents each night.
Ani chayav/chyevet le-havtiach le'atzmi lo lishkoach lomar Laila tov la'horim sheli behchol laila.
אני חייב\חייבת להבטיח לעצמי לא לשכוח לומר לילה טוב להורים שלי בכל לילה.

So why is this so small?
Az lama ze kol-kach katan?
אז למה זה כל כך קטן?

Man - Ish איש
To enter - Le-hikanes - להיכנס
To receive – Lekabel - לקבל
To move (to a place) - La-avore - לעבור
To move (an object) - La-aziz להזיז
Left - Smol שמאל
Right - Yamin ימין
Each / every - Kol כל
Good afternoon - Tza-haraim tovim – צהריים טובים
Different - Acher אחר
Different - shoneh שונה
Throughout - Beh'meshech - בהמשך
Through – Derech - דרך

He is a different man now.
Hoo eesh acher achshav.
הוא איש אחר עכשיו.

I need to move my car because my sister needs to move her things to her car
Ani tza'rich/tz'rei'cha la-aziz et ha mechonit sheli biglal shae achoti tzreicha la-havir et ha-dvarim shela lamechonit shela.
אני צריך\צריכה להזיז את המכונית שלי בגלל שאחותי צריכה להעביר את הדברים שלה למכונית שלה.

I see the sun from the kitchen window throughout the morning.
Ani ro'eh/ro'ha et hashemesh me'chalon ha mitbach bemieshech ha'boker.
אני רוֹאֶה\רוֹאָה את השמש מחלון המטבח במשך הבוקר.

I go into the house from the front entrance and not through the yard.
Ani nichnas la ba'eet mee ha kneesa ha keedmeet ve lo derech ha chatzer.
אני נכנס לבית מהכניסה הקדמית ולא דרך החצר.

To wish - Le'achel - לאחל
Bad – Rah - רע
To get - Lekabel / Lakachat – לקבל\לקחת
To forget – Lishkoach - לשכוח
Everybody – Kulam - כולם
Although – Lamrot - למרות
In front – Lifnei - לפני
To exchange - Le hachlif - להחליף
To change – Leshanot - לשנות
To call – Likro - לקרוא
To sit – Lashevet - לשבת
Brother – Ach - אח
Dad – Aba - אבא
Together – Beyachad - ביחד
Years – Shanim - שנים
Big – Gadol - גדול
Never - Le'olam - לעולם
During – Bezman - בזמן

I want to exchange the money at the bank.
Ani rotze le-hachlif et hakesef ba-bank.
אני רוצה להחליף את הכסף בבנק.

I want to call my brother and my dad today.
Ani rotzeh/rotza lehitkasher le-ach sheli ve le-aba sheli hayom.
אני רוֹצֶה\רוֹצָה להתקשר לאח שלי ולאבא שלי היום.

I don't ever want to see you.
Ani le'olam lo rotze lirot otcha.
אני לעולם לא רוצה לראות אותך.

I don't want to wish you anything bad.
Ani lo rotzeh/rotza le'achel lecha mashehu ra'aa.
אני לא רוֹצֶה\רוֹצָה לאחל לך משהו רע.

I must forget everybody from my past.
Ani chayav/chayevet lishko'ach et koolam mei ha avar.
אני חייב\חייבת לשכוח את כולם מהעבר.

Next (following/after) - Ha'ba - הבא
Next (near/close) - Karov, קרוב
Next (near/close) - Le-yad – ליד
Behind - Me-achor - מאחור
Restaurant - Mis'aada - מסעדה
Bathroom - Shirut-im - שירותים
Bathroom - Chadar ambatya בחדר אמבטיה
See you soon / goodbye - Lehit-raot - להתראות
I must - Ani Chayav – אני חייב
Person - Adaam אדם
Person - Ben adaam בן אדם
Good – Tov - טוב
Which – Eizei - איזה
Area - Ezor איזור
Area - Sviva סביבה

Goodbye my friend.
Leihit'ra'ot chaver.
להתראות חבר.

Which is the best restaurant in the area?
Eezo misada achi tova ba sviva.
איזו מסעדה הכי טובה בסביבה?

I can feel the heat.
Ani yachol lahargeesh et ha chom.
אני יכול להרגיש את החום.

She must get a car before the next year.
Hee tzreicha lekabel mechoniit lifnei ha shana ha'ba'aa.
היא צריכה לקבל מכונית לפני השנה הבאה.

I need to repair a part of the cabinet in the bathroom.
Ani tzarich letaken chelek mei aron ba chadar ambatya.
אני צריך לתקן חלק מהארון בחדר אמבטיה.

Please – Bevakasha - בבקשה
Beautiful - (m)Yafeh - יָפֶה,
Beautiful - (f)yafa - יָפָה
To lift - Le-harim - להרים
Include / Including – Kolel - כולל
Belong – Shayach - שייך
To check – Livdok - לבדוק
Small – Katan - קטן
To feel – Lahargish - להרגיש
Sorry – Slicha - סליחה

I am sorry.
Ani mitzta'er.
אני מצטער

To feel well I must take vitamins.
Kedei lahargeesh tov alai lakachat veetameen'eem.
כדי להרגיש טוב עליי לקחת ויטמינים.

I am near the person that's behind you.
Ani karov l'adam sheh me-achorei'cha/me-achoraeich.
אני קרוב לאדם מֵאֲחוֹרָיךָ\ מֵאֲחוֹרַיִךְ.

We need to check the size of the house.
Anachnu tz'reichim livdok et godel ha-ba'itt.
אנחנו צריכים לבדוק את גודל הבית.

I want to lift this.
Ani rotzei lehareem et zei.
אני רוצה להרים את זה.

Can you please put the wood in the fire?
Ata yachol laseem et ha etz ba'esh?
אתה יכול לשים את העץ באש?

Does the price include everything?
Haiim ha mechir kolel hakol?
האם המחיר כולל הכל?

To hold – Lehachzik - להחזיק
For me – Bishvili - בשבילי
Price – Mechir - מחיר
Real - Amee-tee - אמיתי
Thing – Davar - דבר
Doesn't – Lo - לא
Even though – Lamrot - למרות
Sky – Shamayim - שמיים

Is that a real diamond?
Ha'eem zei yahalom ameet'ee?
האם זה יהלום אמיתי?

This week the weather was very beautiful.
Ha shavua ha-mezeg ha-avir haya mei'od yafeh.
השבוע מזג האויר היה מאוד יפה.

The sun is high in the sky.
Ha shemesh gvoa ba shama'eem.
השמש גבוה בשמיים.

I can pay this although the price is expensive.
Ani yachol leshalem et ze lamrot sheh hamechir gavo'ha.
אני יכול לשלם את זה למרות שהמחיר גבוה.

Can you please hold my hand?
Ata yachol / att yechola lahachzeek lee et ha yad?
אתה יכול\את יכולה להחזיק את היד?

I want to go to sleep.
Ani rotzei/rotza lalechet lishon.
אני רוֹצָה\רוֹצָה ללכת לישון.

Where is the airport?
Eifo sdei ha te'oofa?
איפה שדה התעופה?

Building Bridges

In Building Bridges, we take six conjugated verbs that have been selected after studies I have conducted for several months in order to determine which verbs are most commonly conjugated, and which are then automatically followed by an infinitive verb. For example, once you know how to say, "I need," "I want," "I can," and "I like," you will be able to connect words and say almost anything you want more correctly and understandably. The following three pages contain these six conjugated verbs in first, second, third, fourth, and fifth person, as well as some sample sentences. Please master the entire program up until *here* prior to venturing onto this section.

I need - (m)Ani tzarich – אני צריך
I need - (f) Ani tz'rei'cha – אני צריכה
I want - (m)Ani rotzeh – אני רוֹצֶה
I want - (f)Ani rotza – אני רוֹצָה
I have – (m)Yesh li – יש לי
I have – (f)Yesh li – יש לי
I have to / I must - (m)Ani chayav – אני חייב
I have to / I must - (f)Ani cha'yevet – אני חייבת
I talk - (m)Ani medaber – אני מדבר
I talk - (f)Ani medaberet – אני מדברת

I want to go home.
Ani rotzeh/rotza lalechet habayita.
.אני רוֹצֶה\רוֹצָה ללכת הביתה

I need to find a hospital.
Ani tza'rich/tz'rei'cha limtzo et beit hacholim.
.אני צריך\צריכה למצוא את בית החולים

I need to walk outside the museum.
Ani tzarich lalechet meechootz la mozeihon.
.אני צריך ללכת מחוץ למוזיאון

I am talking with you.
Ani medaber/medaberet itcha/itach.
.אני מדבר\מדברת אִתְּךָ\אִתָּךְ

I can - (m)Ani yachol – אני יכול
I can - (f)Ani yechola – אני יכולה
I go - (m)Ani holech – אני הולך
I go - (f)Ani holechet – אני הולכת
I do - (m)Ani oseh – אני עוֹשֶׂה
I do - (f)Ani osa – אני עוֹשָׂה
I see - (m)Ani ro'eh - אני רוֹאֶה
I see - (f)Ani ro'ha – אני רוֹאָה
I like - (m)Ani o'hev – אני אוהב
I like - (f)Ani o'hevet – אני אוהבת
I say - (m)Ani omer – אני אומר
I say - (f)Ani omeret – אני אומרת

I like to eat oranges.
Ani ohev/ohevet le'echol tapozeem.
אני אוהב\אוהבת לאכול תפוזים.

I can go with you.
Ani yachol/yechola lalechit itcha.
אני יכול\יכולה ללכת איתך.

I am seeing a house today.
Ani ro'eh/ro'ha ba'itt ha-yom.
אני רוֹאֶה\רוֹאָה בית היום.

I am doing this now.
Ani ose/osa et ze achshav.
אני אני עוֹשֶׂה\עוֹשָׂה את זה עכשיו.

I am saying this now.
Ani omer/omeret et ze achshav.
אני אומר\אומרת את זה עכשיו.

Please master *every* single page up until here prior to attempting the following two pages!

(M)You want / do you want?
Atta rotze / haiim atta rotze?
אתה רוֹצֶה \ האם אתה רוצה?

(F) You want / do you want?
Ah'tt rotza / haiim ah'tt rotza?
את רוֹצָה \ האם את רוֹצָה?

He wants / does he want?
Hu rotze / haiim hu rotze?
הוא רוצה \ האם הוא רוצה?

She wants / does she want?
Hee rotza / haiim hee rotza?
היא רוצה \ האם היא רוצה?

(M)We want / do we want?
Anachnu rotzim / Haiim anachnu rotzim?
אנחנו רוצים \ אם אנחנו רוצים?

(F)We want / do we want?
Anachnu rotzot / Haiim anachnu rotzot?
אנחנו רוצות\האם אנחנו רוצות?

(M)They want / do they want?
Hem rotzim / Haiim hem rotzim?
הם רוצים \ האם הם רוצים?

(F)They want / do they want?
Hen rotzot / Haiim hen rotzot?
הן רוצות \ האם הן רוצות?

(M)You (Plural)want/ do you (Pl) want?
Atem rotzim / Haiim atem rotzim?
אתם רוצים \ האם אתם רוצים?

(F)You (pl) want/ do you (Pl) want?
Aten rotzot / Haiim aten rotzot?
אתן רוצות \ האם אתן רוצות ?

(M)You need / do you need?
Atta tzarich / haiim atta tzarich?
אתה צריך \ האם אתה צריך?

(F) You need / do you need?
Ah'tt tzraicha / haiim ah'tt tzraicha?
את צריכה \ האם את צריכה?

He needs / does he need?
Hu tzarich / haiim hu tzarich?
הוא צריך \ האם הוא צריך?

She needs / does she need?
Hee tzraicha / haiim hee tzraicha?
היא צריכה \ האם היא צריכה?

(M)We need / do we need?
Anachnu tzraichim/ Haiim anachnu tzraichim?
אנחנו צריכים \ האם אנחנו צריכים?

(F)We need / do we need?
Anachnu tzraichot / Haiim anachnu tzraichot?
אנחנו צריכות \ האם אנחנו צריכות?

(M)They need / do they need?
Hem tzraichim / Haiim hem tzraichim?
הם צריכים \ האם הם צריכים?

(F)They need / do they need?
Hen tzraichot / Haiim hen tzraichot?
הן צריכות \ האם הן צריכות?

(M)You (Pl)need/ do you (Pl) need?
Atem tzraichim / Haiim atem tzraichim?
אתם צריכים \ האם אתם צריכים?

(F)You (pl)need/ do you (Pl) need?
Aten tzraichot / Haiim aten tzraichot?
אתן צריכות \ האם אתן צריכות?

(M)You can / can you?
Atta yachol / haiim atta yachol?
אתה יכול \ האם אתה יכול?

(F) You can / can you?
Ah'tt yechola / haiim ah'tt yechola?
את יכולה \ האם את יכולה?

He can / can he?
Hu yachol / haiim hu yachol?
הוא יכול \ האם הוא יכול?

She can / can she?
Hee yechola / haiim hee yechola?
היא יכולה \ האם היא יכולה?

(M)We can / can we?
Anachnu yecholim/ Haiim anachnu yecholim?
אנחנו יכולים \ האם אנחנו יכולים?

(F)We can / can we?
Anachnu yecholot / Haiim anachnu yecholot?
אנחנו יכולות \ האם אנחנו יכולות?

(M)They can / can they?
Hem yecholim / Haiim hem yecholim?
הם יכולים \ האם הם יכולים?

(F)They can / can they?
Hen yecholot / Haiim hen yecholot?
הן יכולות \ האם הן יכולות?

(M)You (Pl) can/ can you?
Atem yecholim / Haiim atem yecholim?
אתם יכולים \ האם אתם יכולים?

(F)You (pl) can/ can you?
Aten yecholot / Haiim aten yecholot?
אתן יכולות \ האם אתן יכולות?

(M)You do / do you do?
Atta oseh / haiim atta oseh?
אתה עושה \ האם אתה עושה?

(F) You do / do you do?
Ah'tt osah / haiim ah'tt osah?
את עושה \ האם את עושה?

He does / does he do?
Hu oseh / haiim hu oseh?
הוא עושה \ האם הוא עושה?

She does / does she do?
Hee osah / haiim hee osah?
היא עושה \ האם היא עושה?

(M)We do / do we do?
Anachnu osim/ Haiim anachnu osim?
אנחנו עושים \ האם אנחנו עושים?

(F)We do / do we do?
Anachnu osot / Haiim anachnu osot?
אנחנו עושות \ האם אנחנו עושות?

(M)They do / do they do?
Hem osim / Haiim hem osim?
הם עושים \ האם הם עושים?

(F)They do / do they do?
Hen osot / Haiim hen osot?
הן עושות \ האם הן עושות?

(M)You (Pl) do/ do you (Pl) do?
Atem osim / Haiim atem osim?
אתם עושים \ האם אתם עושים?

(F)You (pl) do/ do you (Pl) do?
Aten osot / Haiim aten osot?
אתן עושות \ האם אתן עושות?

(M)You go / do you go?
Atta holech / haiim atta holech?
?אתה הולך \ האם אתה הולך

(F) You go / do you go?
Ah'tt holechet / haiim ah'tt holechet?
?את הולכת \ האם את הולכת

He goes / does he go?
Hu holech / haiim hu holech?
?הוא הולך \ האם הוא הולך

She goes / does she go?
Hee holechet / haiim hee holechet?
?היא הולכת \ האם היא הולכת

(M)We go / do we go?
Anachnu holchim / Haiim anachnu holchim?
?אנחנו הולכים \ האם אנחנו הולכים

(F)We go / do we go?
Anachnu holchot / Haiim anachnu holchot?
?אנחנו הולכות \ האם אנחנו הולכות

(M)They go / do they go?
Hem holchim / Haiim hem holchim?
?הם הולכים \ האם הם הולכים

(F) They go / do they go?
Hen holchot / Haiim hen holchot?
?הן הולכות \ האם הן הולכות

(M)You (Pl) go/ do you (Pl) go?
Atem holchim / Haiim atem holchim?
?אתם הולכם \ האם אתם הולכים

(F) You (pl) go/ do you (Pl) go?
Aten holchot / Haiim aten holchot?
?אתן הולכות \ האם אתן הולכות

(M)You must / do you have to?
Atta chayav / haiim atta chayav?
אתה חייב \ האם אתה חייב?

(F) You must / do you have to?
Ah'tt chayevet / haiim ah'tt chayevet?
את חייבת \ האם את חייבת?

He must / does he have to?
Hu chayav / haiim hu chayav?
הוא חייב \ האם הוא חייב?

She must / does she have to?
Hee chayevet / haiim hee chayevet?
היא חייבת \ האם היא חייבת?

(M)We must / do we have to?
Anachnu chayavim/ Haiim anachnu chayavim?
אנחנו חייבים \ האם אנחנו חייבם?

(F)We must / do we have to?
Anachnu chayavut / Haiim anachnu chayavut?
אנחנו חייבות \ האם אנחנו חייבות?

(M)They must / do they have to?
Hem chayavim / Haiim hem chayavim?
הם חייבים \ האם הם חייבים?

Do you want to go?
(Male) Haiim atta rotze lalechet?
האם אתה רוצה ללכת?
(Female) Haiim ah'tt rotza lalechet?
האם את רוצה ללכת?

Does he want to fly?
Haiim hu rotze la'oof?
האם הוא רוצה לעוף?

She wants to go to the bus station.
He rotza lalechet le'tachanat ha-otoboos.
היא רוצה ללכת לתחנת האוטובוס.

We want to swim.
(M) Anachnu rotzim lischot.
אנחנו רוצים לשחות.
(F) Anachnu rotzot lischot.
אנחנו רוצות לשחות.

Do they want to run?
(M) Haiim hem rotzim larotz?
האם הם רוצים לרוץ?
(F) Haiim hen rotzot larotz?
האם הן רוצות לרוץ?

Do you need to clean?
Haiim atta tzarich lenakot?
האם אתה צריך לנקות?
Haiim ah'tt tzraicha lenakot?
האם את צריכה לנקות?

She needs to sing a song.
Hee tzraicha lashir shir.
היא צריכה לשיר שיר.

We need to travel.
Anachnu tzrechim letayel.
אנחנו צריכים לטייל.

They don't need to fight.
Hem lo tzraichim lariv.
הם לא צריכים לריב.
Hen lo tzreichot lariv.
הן לא צריכות לריב.

You (plural) need to save your money.
Atemn zreichim lachsoch et ha kesef shelachem.
אתם צריכים לחסוך את הכסף שלהם.
Aten zrei'chot lachsoch et ha kesef shelachen.
אתן צריכות לחסוך את הכסף שלכן.

Can you hear me?
Haiim ata yachol lishmoh'aa oti?
האם אתה יכול לשמוע אותי?
Haiim ah'tt yechola lishmo'aa oti?
האם את יכולה לשמוע אותי?

He can dance very well.
Hu yachol lirkod mei'od tov.
הוא יכול לרקוד מאוד טוב.

We can go out tonight.
Anachnu yecholim latzet halila.
אנחנו יכולים לצאת הלילה.
Anachnu yecholot latzet halila.
אנחנו יכולות לצאת הלילה.

The fireman can break the door during an emergency.
Bezman cheerom ha kaba'eem yecholeem lishbor et ha delet.
בזמן חירום הכבאים יכולים לשבור את הדלת.

Do you like to eat here?
Haiim atta ohev le'echol poe?
האם אתה אוהב לאכול פה?

We like to stay in the house.
Anachnu o'haveem le'ishaher ba ba'iit.
אנחנו אוהבים להשאר בבית.

They like to cook.
Hem ohavim levashel.
הם אוהבים לבשל.
Hen ohavot levashel.
הן אוהבות לבשל.

You (plural) like to play soccer.
Atem oh'haveem lesachek kadoor reg'el.
אתם אוהבים לשחק כדורגל.

Do you go to the movies on weekends?
Ha eem ata olech / att olechet la kolno'a besofei shavoo'a?
האם אתה הולך \ את הולכת לחנות בסופי שבוע?

He goes /fishing.
Hu holech ladoog.
הוא הולך לדוג.

They go out to eat at a restaurant every day.
Em yotzeem la misada kol yom.
הם יוצאים למסעדה כל יום.

Do you have money?
Haiim yesh lecha kesef?
האם יש לךָ כסף?
Haiim yesh lach kesef?
האם יש לךְ כסף?

She must look outside.
Hee chayevet lehistakel hachotza.
היא חייבת להסתכל החוצה.

They have to send the letter.
Hem chayavim lishloach et ha'michtav.
הם חייבים לשלוח את המכתב.

You (plural) have to stand in line.
Atem tzreichim la'amod ba torr.
אתם צריכים לעמוד בתור.

Other Useful Tools in the Hebrew Language

Seasons
Spring – Aviv - אביב
Summer - Kah-yits - קיץ
Autumn – Stav - סתיו
Winter – Choref - חורף

Numbers (Masculine tense)
One – Echad - אחד
Two – Shnaim - שנים
Three – Shlosha - שלושה
Four - Arba'aa - ארבעה
Five – Chamisha - חמישה
Six – Shisha - שישה
Seven - Shiva'aa - שבעה
Eight – Shmona - שְׁמוֹנָה
Nine - Ti-sha'aa - תשעה
Ten - Aasar'aa - עשרה

One boy - Yeled eichad – ילד אחד
Two boys - Shnaei yeladim – שני ילדים
Three boys - Shlosha yeladim – שלושה ילדים
Four boys - Arba-aa yeladim – ארבעה ילדים
Five boys - Chamisha yeladim – חמישה ילדים
Six boys - Shisha yeladim – שישה ילדים
Seven boys - Shiv'aa yeladim – שבעה ילדים
Eight boys - Shmona yeladim – שְׁמוֹנָה ילדים
Nine boys - Tish'aa yeladim – תשעה ילדים
Ten boys - Aasara yeladim – עשרה ילדים

Numbers (Feminine tense)
One – Achat - אחת
Two – Shtaim - שתיים
Three – Shalosh - שלוש
Four – Arba - ארבע
Five – Chamesh - חמש
Six – Shesh - שש
Seven – Sheva - שבע
Eight – Shmoneh - שְׁמוֹנָה
Nine - Taei-sha - תשע
Ten – Eser - עשר

One girl - Yalda achat – ילדה אחת
Two girls - Shtei yeladot – שתי ילדות
Three girls - Shalosh yeladot – שלוש ילדות
Four girls - Arba yeladot – ארבע ילדות
Five girls - Chamesh yeladot – חמש ילדות
Six girls - Shesh yeladot – שש ילדות
Seven girls - Sheva yeladot – שבע ילדות
Eight girls - Shmoneh yeladot – שְׁמוֹנָה ילדות
Nine girls - Taei-sha yeladot – תשע ילדות
Ten girls - Eser yeladot – עשר ילדות

*In the Hebrew Language, when referring to a single noun, the adjective proceeds the noun, example; "one book", *sefer eichad* – ספר אחד. But in plural, the adjective precedes the noun, for example: "two books", *shnaei sfarim* – שני ספרים. When using numbers as adjectives, the conjugation changes, for example: "six books", won't be *shesh sfarim* – שש ספרים, but rather *shisha sfarim* – שישה ספרים.

Days of the Week
Sunday - Yom rishon – יום ראשון
Monday - Yom Sheni – יום שני
Tuesday - Yom Shlishi – יום שלישי
Wednesday - Yom re -ve -ii – יום רביעי
Thursday - Yom Chami shi – יום חמישי
Friday - Yom Shishi – יום שישי
Saturday - Yom Shabat – יום שבת

Colors
Black – Shachor - שחור
White – Lavan - לבן
Gray – A'for - אפור
Red – Adom - אדום
Blue – Kachol - כחול
Yellow - Tsa-hov - צהוב
Green – Yarok - ירוק
Orange – Katom - כתום
Purple – Sagol - סגול
Brown – Chum חום

Cardinal Directions
North – Tzafon - צפון
South – Darom - דרום
East – Mizrach - מזרח
West - Ma'arav - מערב

Conversational Hebrew Quick and Easy

The Most Innovative Technique to Learn the Hebrew Language

Part II

YATIR NITZANY

Translated by:
Semadar Mercedes Friedman

Introduction to the Program

In the first book, you were taught the 350 most useful words in the Hebrew language, which, once memorized, could be combined in order for you to create your own sentences. Now, with the knowledge you have gained, you can use those words in Conversational Hebrew Quick and Easy Part 2 and Part 3, in order to supplement the 350 words that you've already memorized. This combination of words and sentences will help you master the language to even greater proficiency and quicker than with other courses.

The books that comprise Parts 2 and 3 have progressed from just vocabulary and are now split into various categories that are useful in our everyday lives. These categories range from travel to food to school and work, and other similarly broad subjects. In contrast to various other methods, the topics that are covered also contain parts of vocabulary that are not often broached, such as the military, politics, and religion. With these more unusual topics for learning conversational languages, the student can learn quicker and easier. This method is flawless and it has proven itself time and time again.

If you decide to travel to Israel, then this book will help you speak the Hebrew language.

This method has worked for me and thousands of others. It surpasses any other language-learning method system currently on the market today.

This book, Part 2, specifically deals with practical aspects concerning travel, camping, transportation, city living, entertainment such as films, food including vegetables and fruit, shopping, family including grandparents, in-laws, and stepchildren, human anatomy, health, emergencies, and natural disasters, and home situations.

The sentences within each category can help you get by in other countries.

In relation to travel, for example, you are given sentences about food, airport necessities such as immigration, and passports. Helpful phrases include, "Where is the immigration and passport control inside the airport?" and "I want to order a bowl of cereal and toast with jelly." For flights there are informative combinations such as, "There is a long line of passengers in the terminal because of the delay on the runway." When arriving in another country options for what to say include, "We want to hire a driver for the tour. However, we want to pay with a credit card instead of cash" and, "On which street is the car-rental agency.

When discussing entertainment in another country and in a new language, you are provided with sentences and vocabulary that will help you interact with others. You can discuss art galleries and watching foreign films. For example, you may need to say to friends, "I need subtitles if I watch a foreign film" and, 'The mystery-suspense genre films are usually good movies'. You can talk about your own filming experience in front of the camera.

The selection of topics in this book is much wider than in ordinary courses. By including social issue such as incarceration, it will help you to engage with more people who speak the language you are learning.

Part 3 will deal with vocabulary and sentences relevant to indoor matters such as school and the office, but also a variety of professions and sports.

TRAVEL - NESI'YA - נסיעה

Flight – Tissa - טיסה
Airplane – Matos - מטוס
Airport – Sdei te'oofa – שדה תעופה
Terminal - Terminal טרמינל
Terminal – Massof – מסוף
Passport – Darkon - דרכון
Take off (airplane) – Hamra'a - המראה
Landing – Nechita - נחיתה
Departure - Yetzi'a - יציאה
Arrival – Haga'a - הגעה
Gate – Shahar - שער

I enjoy traveling.
Ani (male)nehenei / (female)nehenet linsoa'a.
אני נהנה\נהנת לנסוע.
This is a very expensive flight.
Zot tisa yekara (expensive) me'od.
זאת טיסה יקרה מאוד.
The airplane takes off in the morning and lands at night.
Ha matos mamri baboker ve nochet ba lalila.
המטוס ממריא בבוקר ונוחת בלילה.
We need to go to the departure gate instead of the arrival gate.
Anachnu tzreichim lalechet le-sha'ar ha yetziya bimkom le-shahar haga'a.
אנחנו צריכים ללכת לשער היציאה במקום לשער ההגעה.
What is your final destination?
Ma ha ya'ad ha sof'ee (m)shelcha/(f)shelach?
מה היעד הסופי שֶׁלְךָ\שֶׁלָךְ?
The flight takes off at 3pm, but the boarding commences at 2:20pm.
Ha tissa mamri'a be shalosh achar ha tzo'ha'raim, aval ha aliya la matos matchila be shtaiim ve esriim.
הטיסה ממריאה בשלוש אחר הצהריים, אבל העלייה למטוס מתחילה בשתיים ועשרים.

Luggage – Kvooda - כבודה
Suitcase – Mizvada - מזוודה
Baggage claim - Issuf ha kvuda – איסוף הכבודה
Customs – Meches - מכס
Passenger – **(Male)** Nosae'ha - נוסע
Passenger – **(Female)** Nosa'att - נוסעת
Passport control - Piku'ach ha darkoniim - פיקוח הדרכונים
Final Destination – Ya'ad sof'ee – יעד סופי
Boarding - Aliya la matos – עלייה למטוס
Runway – Maslool - מסלול
Line – Shura - שורה
Delay – Ikoov - עיקוב
Wing – Kanaf - כנף

My suitcase is at the baggage claim.
Ha mizvada sheli nimtzet be issuf ha kvuda.
המזוודה שלי נמצאת באיסוף הכבודה.

I am almost finished at customs.
Kimaat si'yamti (finished) eim ha meches.
כמעט סיימתי עם המכס.

I don't like to sit above the wing of the airplane.
Ani lo (m)ohev/(f)ohevet lashevet mehal knaf ha matos.
אני לא אוהב\אוהבת לשבת מעל כנף המטוס.

There is a long line of passengers in the terminal because of the delay on the runway.
Ba-i'kvot (because of) ha i'koov ba maslool Yesh shura aruka shel nosyiim mipnei.
בעקבות העיקוב במסלול יש שורה ארוכה של נוסעים לפני.

Where is the passport control inside the airport?
Eifo piku'ach ha darkoniim be sdei ha te'oofa.
איפה פיקוח הדרכונים בשדה התעופה?

International flight – Tissa bein lehumit – טיסה בין לאומית
Domestic flight – Tissat pniim – טיסת פנים
Business class – Machlekat a'asakiim – מחלקת העסקים
First class – Machlaka rishona – מחלקה ראשונה
Economy class – Machleket ta'ya'riim - מחלקת תיירים
Business trip - Nesiy'at hasakiim – נסיעת עסקים
Round trip - Tissa haloch va shov – טיסה הלוך ושוב
Direct flight - Tiisa yeshira – טיסה ישירה
One-way flight - Tissa lekivun echad – טיסה לכיוון אחד
Return flight - Tiisa't chazara – טיסת חזרה
Flight attendant - (F) Dayelet - דיילת
Flight attendant - (M)dayal - דייל
Reservation – Hazmana - הזמנה

For international flights, you must be at the airport at least three hours before the flight.
Letisot bein-le'umiyot atem/aten chayavim/chayavot lihyot beesdei ha te'oofa lefachot shalosh sha'ott lifnei ha tissa.
לטיסות בין לאומיות אתם\אתן חייבים\חייבות להיות בשדה התעופה לפחות שלוש שעות לפני הטיסה.

For a domestic flight, I need to arrive at the airport at least two hours before the flight.
Le tisot pnimiyot ani (m)tzarich/(f)tzreicha lihyot beesdei ha te'oofa lefachot sha'ataim lifnei ha tissa.
לטיסות פנימיות אני צריך\צריכה להיות בשדה התעופה לפחות שעתיים לפני הטיסה.

Business class is usually cheaper than first class.
Machleket a'asakim bederech'klal (usually) yoter zola (cheaper) mi ha machlaka ha rishona.
מחלקת העסקים בדרך כלל יותר זולה ממחלקה ראשונה.

A one-way ticket is cheaper than the round-trip ticket at the travel agency.
Kartiss lekivun echad zol yoter mae kartiss aloch vashov bee sochnut ha nesiyot.
כרטיס לכיוון אחד זול יותר מכרטיס הלוך ושוב בסוכנות הנסיעות.

Layover - Chibur tissa – חיבור טיסה
Connection - kishoor tissa – קישור טיסה
Security check – Bdika bitchoniit – בדיקה ביטחונית
Check in counter – Dalpaak ha kabala – דלפק הקבלה
Checked bags - Tikiim la matos – תיקים למטוס
Carry-on bag - Tikei yaad – תיקי יד
Travel agency - Sochnut nesiyot - סוכנות נסיעות
Travel agency - Misrad nesiyot – משרד נסיעות
Visa - A'shrat-knissa – אשרת כניסה
Temporary visa – A'shrat knissa zmanit – אשרת כניסה זמנית
Temporary visa – visa zmanit – ויזה זמנית
Permanent visa – A'shrat knissa kvu'ha – אשרת כניסה קבועה
Permanent visa – visa kvu'ha – ויזה קבועה
Country – Eretz - ארץ

I prefer a direct flight without a layover.
Ani ma'adiif tissa yeshira lelo chibur.
.אני מעדיף טיסה ישירה ללא חיבור

I must reserve my return flight.
Alai lehazmin et tissat ha chazara sheli.
.עליי להזמין את טיסת החזרה שלי

Why do I need to remove my shoes at the security check?
Lama ani tzarich/tzreicha lachalotz nahalaiim bee vdikat ha bitachon?
?למה אני צריך\צריכה לחלוץ נעליים בבדיקת הביטחון

I have three checked bags and one carry-on.
Yesh li shalosh mizvadot ve tik yad echad.
.יש לי שלוש מזוודות ותיק יד אחד

I have to ask my travel agent if this country requires a visa.
Ani tzarich lish'ol et sochen ha nesyot sheli iim ha eretz hazot doreshet a'shrat-knissa.
.אני צריך לשאול את סוכן הנסיעות שלי האם המדינה הזאת דורשת אשרת כניסה

The flight attendant told me to go to the check in counter.
Ha dayelet amra li lalechet le dalpak ha kabala.
.הדיילת אמרה לי ללכת לדלפק הקבלה

Trip – Nessi'ya נסיעה
Trip – Ti'yool – טיול
Tourist – Tayar - תייר
Tourism – Tayaroot - תיירות
Holiday – Chag - חג
Leisure – Pnaei - פנאי
Vacations – Choofsha - חופשה
Currency exchange - Hamarat matbae'a – המרת מטבע
Port of entry - Namal hakniisa – נמל הכניסה
Car rental agency - Sochnoot haskarat mechoniyot – סוכנות השכרת מכוניות
Identification - Te'oodat zehoot – תעודת זהות
Road - Kviish כביש
Road - Derech דרך
Road - Maslool מסלו
Map – Mapa - מפה

I had an amazing trip.
Haya li ti'yool mae'hamem (amazing).
.היה לי טיול מהמם

The currency exchange counter is past the port of entry.
Dalpak hamraat matbei'a hu nimtza achrei atar ha kniisa.
.דלפק המרת המטבע הוא נמצא אחרי אתר הכניסה

There is a lot of tourism during the holidays and vacations.
Yesh harbei tayariim bezmaan ha chaggiim ve ha choofsh'ot.
.יש הרבה תיירים בזמן החגים והחופשות

Where is the car-rental agency?
Eifo ha sochnoot le haskarat rechev?
?איפה הסוכנות להשכרת רכב

You need to show your identification.
Ata/aat tzarich/tzreicha lahar'ott et tehudat hazehoot shelcha/shelach.
.אתה\את צריך\צריכה להראות את תעודת הזהות שֶׁלְךָ\שֶׁלָךְ

It's more convenient to use the GPS on the roads instead of a map.
Ze yoter no'ach lehishtamesh ba gps al ha kvishiim mehasher ba-mapa.
.זה יותר נוח להשתמש בג'יפיאס על הכבישים מאשר במפה

Information center - Merkaz meida'a – מרכז מידע
Bank – Banc - בנק
Hotel – Beit malon – בית מלון
Motel – Malon - מלון
Hostel - Achsan'ee'ya - אכסנייה
Driver – **(Male)** Ne'hag - נהג
Driver – **(Female)** Na'hegget - נהגת
Credit - Ashrai - אשראי
Cash – Mezuman - מזומן
GPS – GPS – ג'יפיאס
A guide - **(M)**Madrich - מדריך
A guide - **(F)**madricha - מדריכה
Tour - Si'yoor - סיור
Ski resort - Atar ski – אתר סקי

Why is the information center closed today?
Madoo'a merkaz ha meida sagur hayom?
מדוע מרכז המידע סגור היום?

When I am in a foreign country, I go to the bank before I go to the hotel.
Ka'asher ani ba-eretz zara (foreign) ani kodem holech/holechet la banc lifnei shae ani holech/holechet la malon.
כאשר אני בארץ זרה אני קודם הולך\הולכת לבנק לפני שאני הולך\הולכת למלון.

I need to book my leisure vacation at the ski resort today.
Hayom ani tzariich lahazmin et choofshat ha menucha sheli ba atar ha skii.
היום אני צריך להזמין את חופשת המנוחה שלי באתר הסקי.

We want to hire a driver for the tour.
Anachnu rotziim liskor na'hag la'siyur.
אנחנו רוצים לשכור נהג לסיור.

We want to pay with a credit card instead of cash.
Anachnu rotzim/rotzot leshalem bae-kartiis (card) ashrai bimkom bee-mezuman.
אנחנו רוצים\רוצות לשלם בכרטיס אשראי במקום במזומן.

Does the tour include an English-speaking guide?
Ha'iim ha siyur kolel (include) madrich/madricha doverr/doveret angliit?
האם הסיור כולל מדריך\מדריכה דובר\דוברת אנגלית?

TRANSPORTATION – TACHBURA - תחבורה

Car - Mechonit -מכונית
Car - Oto -אוטו
Car - Rechev -רכב
Train – Rakevet - רכבת
Train station - Tachanat rakevet - תחנת רכבת
Train tracks - Pasei rakevet – פסי רכבת
Train cart - Kar'onn rakevet – קרון רכבת
Taxi – Moniit - מונית
Subway - Rakevet tachtit – רכבת תחתית
Motorcycle - Ofno'a – אופנוע
Scooter - Katno'a – קטנוע
Station – Tachana - תחנה

Where is the public transportation?
Eifo ha tachbura ha tziburit?
איפה התחבורה הציבורית?

Where can I buy a bus ticket?
Eifo ani (m)yachol/(f)yechola liknot kartis otoboos?
איפה אני יכול\יכולה לקנות כרטיס אוטובוס?

Please call a taxi.
Bevakasha tazmin moniit.
בבקשה תזמין מונית

In some cities, you don't need a car because you can rely on the subway.
Bae a'ariim mesuyamot (certain) ata/att lo tzariich/tzreicha mechoniit ki ata/att yachol/yechola lismoch (rely) al ha rakevet ha tachtit.
בערים מסוימות אתה\את לא צריך\צריכה מכונית כי אתה\את יכול\יכולה לסמוך על הרכבת התחתית.

Where is the train station?
Eifo tachanat ha rakevet?
איפה תחנת הרכבת?

The train cart is still stuck on the tracks.
Ha karon adaiin (still) takua (stuck) al pasei ha rakevet.
הקרון עדיין תקוע על פסי הרכבת.

Helicopter – Masok - מסוק
Bus – Otoboos - אוטובוס
School bus – Otoboos beit ha sefer – אוטובוס בית ספר
Limousine – Limosina – לימוזינה
Driver license - Rishayon ne'hee'ga – רישיון נהיגה
Vehicle registration - Rishum rechev – רישיון רכב
Car insurance - Beetuach rechev – ביטוח רכב
License plate - Luchit rishui – לוחית רישוי
Ticket – Kartis - כרטיס
Ticket (penalty) – Knass - קנס

The motorcycles make loud noises.
Ha ofnoiim mar'ishiim (noisy) me'od.
האופנועים מרעישים מאוד.

Where can I rent a scooter?
Eifo ani yachol/yechola liskor katno'a?
איפה אני יכול\יכולה לשכור קטנוע?

I want to plan a helicopter tour.
Ani (m)rotzei/(f)rotza letachnen (to plan) si'yoor bamasok.
אני רוֹצֶה\רוֹצָה לתכנן סיור במסוק.

I want to go to the party in a limousine.
Ani rotzei/rotza lalechet la mesiba (party) bae moniit.
אני רוֹצֶה\רוֹצָה ללכת למסיבה במונית.

Don't forget to bring your driver's license and registration.
Al tishkach/tishkachi lahavi et rishayon ha nehiga ve et rishum ha rechev shelcha/shelach.
אל תשכח \ תשכחי להביא את רישיון הנהיגה ואת רישום הרכב שֶׁלְּךָ\שֶׁלָּךְ.

The cop gave me a ticket because my license plate has expired.
Ha shoterr het'eel (imposed) a'lai knaas ki luchit ha rishui sheli lo hayta betokef.
השוטר הטיל עליי קנס כי לוחית הרישוי שלי לא הייתה בתוקף.

Truck – Masahiit - משאית
Pickup truck – Tenderr - טנדר
Bicycle – Ofanaiim - אופניים
Van – Vann - וואן
Gas station – Tachanat delek – תחנת דלק
Gasoline - Delek דלק
Gasoline benzin – בנזין
Tire - Tzamiig צמיג -
Tire - Galgal – גלגל
Oil change – Hachlafat shmaniim – החלפת שמנים
Tire change – Hachlafat tzmiggim - החלפת צמיגים
Mechanic – Mechona'ee - מכונאי

I can put my bicycle in my truck.
Ani yachol/yechola lasiim et ha ofanaiim sheli ba masa'iit.
אני יכול \ יכולה לשים את האופניים שלי במשאית?

Where is the gas station?
Eifo tachanat ha delek?
איפה תחנת הדלק?

I need gasoline and also to put air in my tires.
Ani tzarich delek ve lemal'ae (to fill) aviir (air) ba zmigg'im.
אני צריך דלק ולמלא אוויר בצמיגים.

I need to take my car to the mechanic for a tire and oil change.
Ani tzarich lakachat et ha mechoniit sheli la mechona'ee lehachlafat tzmiggim ve shmaniim.
אני צריך לקחת את המכונית שלי למכונאי להחלפת צמיגים ושמנים.

I can put my canoe in the van.
Ani yachol/yechola lasiim et ha kanu ba van.
אני יכול\יכולה לשים את הקאנו בוואן.

Can I bring my yacht to the boat show at the marina?
Haiim ani yachol/yechola lahavi et ha yachta sheli lemofa (show) sirot ba marina?
האם אני יכול\יכולה להביא את היאכטה שלי למופע סירות במרינה?

Canoe – Kanu - קאנו
Ship – Sfina - ספינה
Boat – Siraa - סירה
Yacht – Yachta - יאכטה
Sailboat - Sirat mifras – סירת מפרש
Sailboat - Mifrasiit - מפרשית
Motorboat - Siraat mano'a – סירת מנוע
Marina – Marinna - מרינה
The dock - Ha mezach - המזח
Cruise - Sha'ee'eet - שייט
Cruise ship - Sfinaat sha'ee'eet – ספינת שייט
Ferry - Ma'aboret - מעבורת
Submarine – Tzolelet - צוללת

I prefer a motorboat instead of a sailboat.
Ani ma'adif/ma'adifa siraat mano'a a'al sirat mifrasiim.
אני מעדיף\מעדיפה סירת מנוע על סירת מפרש.
I want to leave my boat at the dock on the island.
Ani rotzei/rotza lahash'iir et ha siraa sheli bamezach shel ha iee (island).
אני רוֹצֶה\רוֹצָה את הסירה שלי במזח של האי.
This spot is a popular stopping point for the cruise ship.
Ha nekuda (spot) hazot hee nekuda me'od populareet (popular) avor sfinot ha sha'ee'eet.
הנקודה הזאת היא נקודה מאוד פופולרית עבור ספינות השייטת.
This was an excellent cruise.
Ze haya shahit metzuyan.
זה היה שייט מצוין.
Do you have the schedule for the ferry?
Yesh lecha/lach et luach-ha-zmaniim (the schedule) shel ha ma'aboret.
יש לְךָ\לָךְ את לוח הזמנים של המעבורת?
The submarine is yellow.
Ha tzolelet hee tzehooba.
הצוללת היא צהובה.

CITY – IIR - עיר

Town - A'yara - עיירה
Village – Kfar - כפר
House – Ba'iit - בית
Home – Ba'iit - בית
Apartment – Dira - דירה
Building - Binyan - בניין
Highrise building - Binyan rav komot - בניין רב קומות
Skyscraper – Gored shchakiim – גורד שחקים
Tower – Migdal - מגדל
Neighborhood – Shchuna - שכונה

Is this a city or a village?
Ha'iim zot iir o kfar?
?האם זאת עיר או כפר

Does he live in a house or an apartment?
Ha'iim hu gar be ba'iit pratii (private) o bedira?
?האם הוא גר בבית פרטי או בדירה

This residential building does not have an elevator, just stairs.
Bae binyan ha megurim hazei ein ma'aliit, raak madregot.
בבניין המגורים הזה אין מעלית, רק מדרגות.

These skyscrapers are located in the center city.
Gordei ha shchakiim nimtza'eem bae merkaz ha iir.
גורדי השחקים נמצאים במרכז העיר.

The tower is tall but the building beside it is very short.
Ha migdal gavoha aval ha binyan letzido me'od namuch.
המגדל גבוה אבל הבניין לצידו מאוד נמוך.

This is a beautiful neighborhood.
Zohee schoona yafa.
זוהי שכונה יפה.

There is a fence around the construction site.
Yesh gader misaviv la atar ha bniiya.
יש גדר מסביב לאתר בנייה.

Office building – Binyan misradiim – בניין משרדים
Post office – Ha dohar - הדואר
Location - Makom מקום
Location - Atar – אתר
Elevator – Ma'aliit - מעלית
Stairs – Madregot - מדרגות
Fence – Gader - גדר
Construction site – Atar bniiya – אתר בנייה
Bridge – Gesher - גשר
Gate - Sha'ar - שער
City hall – Iri'ya - עירייה
Mayor - Rosh ha iir – ראש העיר
Fire department – Mechabei esh – מכבי אש
Pedestrians – Olchei reg'el – הולכי רגל
Crosswalk - Ma'avar chatzaya – מעבר חציה

The post office is located in that office building.
Ha'dohar nimtza ba binyan ha misradim hazei.
הדואר נמצא בבניין המשרדים הזה.

The bridge is closed today.
Ha'ggesher saguur (closed) hayom.
הגשר סגור היום.

The gate is open.
Ha sha'ar patuach.
השער פתוח.

The fire department is located in the building next to city hall.
Binyan mechabei ha'esh nimtza ba binyan leyad ha iri'ya.
בניין מכבי האש נמצא בבניין ליד העירייה.

The mayor of Tel Aviv is very well known.
Rosh ha iir shel tel aviv me'od yadooa.
ראש העיר של תל אביב מאוד ידוע.

The pedestrians use the crosswalk to cross the road.
Chotzei ha reg'el mishtamsh'eem bae mahavar ha chatzaya kedei lachtzot et ha kvish.
חוצי הרגל משתמשים במעבר החציה כדי לחצות את הכביש.

Street – Rechov - רחוב
Main street - Rechov ha rashi – רחוב הראשי
To park – Lachanot - לחנות
Parking - Chanaya חנייה
Parking lot - Migrash chanaya – מגרש חנייה
Sidewalk – Midracha - מדרכה
Traffic - Tnoo'a תנועה
Traffic Tachbura (also means transportation) - תחבורה
Traffic light – Ramzor - רמזור
Red (traffic) light – Ramzor adom – רמזור אדום
Yellow (traffic) light - Ramzor tzahov – רמזור צהוב
Green (traffic) light – Ramzor yarok – רמזור ירוק

The parking is on the main street and not on the sidewalk.
Ha chanaya ba rechov ha rashi ve lo ba midracha.
החנייה ברחוב הראשי ולא על המדרכה.

Where is the parking lot?
Eifo migrash ha chanaya?
איפה מגרש החנייה?

The traffic is very bad today.
Ha tnu'ha groo'a (bad) me'od hayom.
התנועה גרועה מאוד היום.

You must avoid the fast lane because it's a toll lane.
Ata tzarich lehimana mi ha natiiv hamaiir mikivaan shae ze nativ agrat.
אתה צריך להמנע מהנתיב המהיר מכיוון שזה נתיב אגרה.

We don't like to drive on the highway.
Anachnu lo ohavim linhogg (to drive) al ha kvish ha rashi.
אנחנו לא אוהבים לנהוג על הכביש הראשי.

At a red light you need to stop, at a yellow light you must be prepared to stop and at a green you can drive.
Bei orr adom tzarich lahatzor, bei orr tzahov mitkonenim lahatzor, ve bei orr yarok nossii'm.
באור אדום צריך לעצור, באור צהוב מתכוננים לעצור, באור ירוק נוסעים.

This road has too many traffic lights.
Ba rechov hazei yesh yoter-mi'daii (too many) ramzoriim.
ברחוב הזה יש יותר מידי רמזורים.

Lane - Natiiv -נתיב
Lane - Maslul – מסלול
Toll lane - Agrat maslool – אגרת מסלול
Fast lane – Natiiv mahiir – נתיב מהיר
Slow lane – Maslul itii – מסלול איטי
Right lane – Natiiv yemani – נתיב ימני
Left lane – Natiiv smoli – נתיב שמאלי.
Highway – Kvish rashi – כביש ראשי
Intersection - Tzomet צומת
Intersection - michlaf – מחלף
U-turn - Parsa - פרסה
Tunnel – Minhara - מנהרה
Shortcut – Kitzoor derecho – קיצור דרך
Bypass - Ma'akaf - מעקף
Stop sign - Tamroor atzira – תמרור עצירה

At the intersection, we need to stay in the left lane instead of the right lane because that's a bus lane.
Batzomet tzrichim lehishaher ba maslul smali bimkom ba maslul ha yimini kii ha maslul ha yimini ze maslul otobosiim.
בצומת צריכים להישאר במסלול השמאלי במקום במסלול הימיני כי המסלול הימיני זה מסלול אוטובוסים.

The tunnel seems longer than yesterday.
Ha minhara neer'et arooka yoter mi etmol.
המנהרה נראת ארוכה יותר מאתמול.

It's a short drive.
Zo nesyia ktzara.
זו נסיעה קצרה.

The next bus stop is far away from here.
Tachanat ha otoboos haba'ha rechoka mikan.
תחנת האוטובוס הבאה רחוקה מכאן.

You need to turn right at the stop sign and then continue on straight.
Ata tzarich/tzreicha lifnot yemeena bae tamroor ha atzira ve az lahamshich yashar.
אתה צריך\צריכה לפנות ימינה בתמרור העצירה ואז להמשיך ישר.

Capital – Iir habira – עיר הבירה
Resort - Atar nofesh – אתר נופש
Port – Nemal - נמל
Road – Kvish - כביש
Trail, path – Shveel – שביל
Bus station - Tachanat otoboos – תחנת אוטובוס
Bus stop – Tachanat otoboos – תחנת אוטובוס
Night club – Mo'adon Layla – מועדון לילה
Downtown – Merkaz ha'iir – מרכז העיר
District - Rova'a - רובע
Statue - Pesel - פסל
Monument – Andarta - אנדרטה
Castle – Armon - ארמון

The capital is a major attraction point for tourists.
Habira hee nekudat-meshicha merkaziit le tayariim.
הבירה היא נקודת משיכה מרכזית לתיירים.

The resort is next to the port.
Atar ha nofesh hu leyad ha namal.
אתר הנופש הוא ליד הנמל.

The night club is located in the downtown area.
Mo'adon ha laila nimtza ba merkaz ha iir.
מועדון הלילה נמצא במרכז העיר.

In which district do you live in?
Bei eize rova'a ata gar?
באיזה רובע אתה גר?

This statue is a city monument.
Ha pesel hu andarta shel ha iir.
הפסל הוא אנדרטה של העיר.

This is an ancient castle.
Ze armon aatik.
זה ארמון עתיק.

Synagogue - Beit kneest – בית כנסת
Church - Knei'si'ya - כנסיה
Cathedral - Catedrala - קתדרלה
Mosque - Meesgad מיסגד
Science museum – Mo'ze'onn mada'a – מוזיאון מדע
Zoo – Gan chayot – גן חיות
Playground – Gan sha'ha'shu'iim גן שעשועים
Playground – Gan mischakim גן משחקים
Swimming pool – Breicha - בריכה
County – Machoz - מחוז
Jail – Beit ha ke'lei – בית הכלא
Prison - Beit ha sohar – בית הסוהר

Where is the local synagogue?
Eifo beit ha kneset ha mekomi?
איפה בית הכנסת המקומי?
That is a beautiful cathedral.
Zo catedrala yafa.
זה קתדרלה יפה.
Do you want to go to the zoo or the science museum?
Hayiim ata/att rotza/rotze lalechet la gan chayot o le mo'ze'onn ha mada'a?
האם אתה\את רוֹצֶה\ רוֹצָה ללכת לגן חיות או למוזיאון המדע?
The children are in the playground.
Ha yeladim bei gan ha mischakim.
הילדים בגן המשחקים.
The swimming pool is closed for the community today.
Brechat ha schee'ya sgura hayom la kahal.
בריכת השחייה סגורה היום לקהל.
You need to follow the trail alongside the main street to reach the bus station.
Ata\att tzarich/tzreicha la'akov acharie ha shvil letzad harechov ha rashi kedei lahagiya le tachanat ha otoboos.
אתה\את צריך\צריכה לעקוב אחרי השביל לצד הרחוב הראשי כדי להגיע לתחנת האוטובוס.
There is a jail in this county, but not a prison.
Yesh beit ke'lei ba machoz azei, aval ein beit sohar.
יש בית כלא במחוז הזה, אבל אין בית סוהר.

ENTERTAINMENT – BIDUR - בידור

Film / movie – Seret - סרט
Theater (movie theater) - Kolno'a - קולנוע
Actor – Sachkan - שחקן
Actress – Sachkaniit - שחקנית
Genre – Genre – ז'אנר
Subtitles – Ktoo'vi'yot - כתוביות
Action film - Seret pe'ula – סרט פעולה
Foreign film - Seret zaar – סרט זר
Suspense film – Seret metach – סרט מתח
Documentary film - Seret te'oodati – סרט תיעודתי
Documentary film - Dokumentari – דוקומנטרי

There are three new movies at the theater that I want to see.
Yesh shlosha sratiim chadashim ba kolno'a shae ani rotze/rotza lir'ott.
יש שלושה סרטים חדשים בקולנוע שאני רוֹצֶה\ רוֹצָה לראות.

He is a really good actor.
Hu sachkan mamash tov.
הוא שחקן ממש טוב.

She is an excellent actress
Hee sachkanit metzu'yenet.
היא שחקנית מצוינת.

That was a good action movie
Ze haya seret pe'ola tov.
זה היה סרט פעולה טוב.

We need subtitles if we watch a foreign film.
Anu tzrichiim ktuviyot iim anu tzofiim bei seret zaar.
אנו צריכים כתוביות אם אנו צופים בסרט זר.

Mystery or suspense films are usually good movies.
Sirtei metach o mistoriim hem bederech klal sratiim toviim.
סרטי מתח או מסתוריים הם בדרך כלל סרטים טובים.

I like documentary films. However, comedy-drama or romance films are better.
Ani hohev/hohevet seertei te'oodah, aval sirtei comedia-drama o sireti romanti hem yoter mehaniim (enjoyable).
אני אוהב\אוהבת סרטי תעודה, אבל סרטי קומדיה-דרמה או סרטי רומנטי הם יותר מהנים.

Biography - Toldot cha'eem – תולדות חיים
Drama film - Seret drama – סרט דרמה
Comedy film - Seret comedia – סרט קומדיה
Romance film - Seret romantika – סרט רומנטיקה
Horror film - Seret ay'ma – סרט אימה
Animation film - Seret animatziya – סרט אנימציה
Animation film - Seret hitool'ee – סרט היתולי
Cartoon – Seret metzooyar – סרט מצוייר
Director – Bamai - במאי
Producer – Mefiik - מפיק
Audience – Ka'hal - קהל
Television – Televisya - טלוויזיה
A show (as in television) – Tochnit - תוכנית
A show (as in live performance) - Hofa'a – הופעה
Channel – Arutz - ערוץ
Series (in television) – Sidra - סדרה
Episode – Chelek - חלק

Sometimes biographies are boring to watch.
Litzpot bae toldot cha'eem lefamim ze me'sha'ha'mem.
.לצפות בתולדות חיים לפעמים זה משעמם
I like to watch horror movies.
Ani ohev/ohevet lir'ott sirtei eima.
.אני אוהב\אוהבת לראות סרטי אימה
It's fun to watch animated movies.
Naiim litzpot bae srat'eem hitooli'eem.
נעים לצפות בסרטים היתוליים
The director and the producer can meet the audience today.
Ha bamai ve ha mafiik yecholiim lifgosh et ha ka'hal hayome.
.הבמאי והמפיק יכולים לפגוש את הקהל היום
It's time to buy a new television.
Heg'ee'ya hazman liknot televisia chadasha.
.הגיע הזמן לקנות טלוויזיה חדשה
This was the first episode of this television show yet it was a long series.
Ze haya haperek harishon shel sidrat ha televisya ha zot, ve zot hayta sidra aruka.
.זה היה הפרק הראשון של סדרת הטלוויזיה הזאת, וזאת הייתה סדרה ארוכה

News – Chadashot - חדשות
News station – Tachanat chadashot – תחנת חדשות
Screening - Hak'rana - הקרנה
Live broadcast - Shidoor yashiir – שידור ישיר
Live broadcast - Shidur cha'yee – שידור חי
Broadcast – Shidoor - שידור
Headline – Kotarot - כותרת
Viewer – Tzofae - צופה
Speech – Ne'oom - נאום
Script – Tasriit - תסריט
Screen – Masach - תסריט
Camera – Matzlema - מצלמה
Commercial – Pirsomet - פרסומת
Anchorman – Shadran - שדרן
Anchorwoman - Shadran'eet - שדרנית

There aren't any commercials on this channel.
Eiin pirsomot ba arutz hazei.
אין פרסומות בערוץ הזה.

They decided to screen a live broadcast on the news.
Hem echlit'oo lehakreen shidur yashiir ba chadashot.
הם החליטו להקרין שידור ישיר בחדשות.

The news station featured the headlines before the program began.
Tachanat ha chadashot hekrina et hakotarot lifnei atchalat ha tochnit.
תחנת החדשות הקרינה את הכותרות לפני התחלת התוכנית.

Tonight, all the details about the incident were mentioned on the news.
Ha laila, kol ha prat'eem shel ha mikrei hoozker'oo ba chadashot.
הלילה, כל הפרטים של המקרה הוזכרו בחדשות.

The viewers wanted to hear the presidential speech today.
Ha tzofim ratzu lishmo'a et ne'oom ha nasii (president) hayom.
הצופים רצו לשמוע את נאום הנשיא היום.

I must read my script in front of the screen and the camera
Ani chayav/chayevet likro et ha tasriit sheli mool ha masach ve ha matzlema.
אני חייב\חייבת לקרוא את התסריט שלי מול המסך והמצלמה.

Theater (play) – Tae'atron - תיאטרון
A musical - Machaz'zemer - מחזמר
A play - Machazei - מחזה
A play - Hatzaga – הצגה
Stage – Bama - במה
Audition - Mivchan bama – מבחן במה
Performance – Hofa'a - הופעה
Box office – Kupa - קופה
Ticket – Kartis - כרטיס
Singer – **(M)** Zamar – זמר
Singer – **(F)** Zameret זמרת
Band – Lae'haka - להקה
Orchestra – Tizmoret - תזמורת
Opera – Ópaera - אופרה

It was a great musical performance.
Ze haya machaz'zemer nehedar.
.זה היה מחזמר נהדר

Can I perform for the play on this stage?
Ani yachol/yechola lehofi'ya ba machazae al habama hazot?
אני יכול\יכולה להופיע במחזה על הבמה הזאת?

She is the lead singer of the band.
Hee ha zameret ha rasheet (the lead) shel ha lehaka.
.היא הזמרת הראשית של הלהקה

I will go to the box office tomorrow to purchase tickets for the opera.
Ani elech la kupa machar kede'ee liknot kartisim la opaera.
.אני אלך לקופה מחר כדי לקנות כרטיסים לאופרה

The orchestra needs to perform below the stage.
Ha tizmoret tzriecha lenagen mitachat la bama.
.התזמורת צריכה לנגן מתחת לבמה

We want to enjoy the entertainment this evening.
Anachnu rotzim lehenot mae ha bidur ha erev (evening).
.אנחנו רוצים להנות מהבידור הערב

Music – Musica - מוזיקה
Song – Shiir - שיר
Musical instrument – Klei neg'ina – כלי נגינה
Drum – Toff - תוף
Guitar – Guitarra - גיטרה
Piano – Psanter - פסנתר
Trumpet – Cha'tzo'tzra - חצוצרה
Violin – Kinor - כינור
Flute – Chalil - חליל
Art – Omanoot - אומנות
Gallery – Galerya - גלריה
Studio - Oolpan – אולפן
Studio - Stoodyo – סטודיו
Museum – Musae'on - מוזיאון

I like to listen to this type of music. I hope to hear a good song.
Ani ohev/ohevet le'ha'aziin la soog hazei shel musica. Ani mekavei/mekava lishmo'a shiir tov.
.אני אוהב\אוהבת להאזין לסוג הזה של מוזיקה. אני מְקַוֶּה\מְקַוָּה לשמוע שיר טוב

The common musical instruments that are used in a concert are drums, guitars, pianos, trumpets, violins, and flutes.
Ba konsert, klei ha neg'ina ha nefotzim beyoter hem tup'iim, guitarot, psanterim, chatzo'zrot, kinorot, ve chalilim.
בקונצרט, כלי הנגינה הנפוצים ביותר הם תופים, גיטרות, פסנתרים, חצוצרות, כינורות וחלילים.

The art gallery has a studio for rent.
Le galeriat ha omanoot yesh oolpan le haskara.
.לגלריית האומנות יש אולפן להשכרה

I went to an art museum yesterday.
Halachti le musae'on omanoot etmol.
הלכתי למוזיאון אומנות אתמול

FOOD - MAZON - OCHEL - אוכל

Grocery store – Makolet - מכולת
Market – Shook - שוק
Supermarket - Supermarket – סופרמרקט
Supermarket - Super - סופר
Groceries - Metzrachei ochel – מצרכי אוכל
Butcher shop – Atleez - אטליז
Butcher – Katsav - קצב
Bakery - Ma-afia – מאפייה
Baker – Ofae - אופה
Breakfast – Aruchat boker – ארוחת בוקר
Lunch – Aruchat tzohoraiim – ארוחת צהריים
Dinner – Aruchat erev – ארוחת ערב
Meat – Basar - בשר
Chicken – Off - עוף
Seafood – Peirot yam – פירות ים

Where is the nearest grocery store?
Eifo ha makolet ha krova beyoter?
איפה המכולת הקרובה ביותר?
Where can I buy meat and chicken?
Eifo ochal liknot basar ve off?
איפה אוכל לקנות בשר ועוף?
The butcher shop is near the bakery.
Ha atleez nimtza besamooch la ma-afia.
האטליז נמצא בסמוך למאפייה.
I have to go to the market, to buy a half kilo of meat.
Ani tzarich/tzreicha lalechet la shook kedei liknot chatzi kilo basar.
אני צריך\צריכה ללכת לשוק כדי לקנות חצי קילו בשר.
The groceries are already in the car.
Metzrachei ha mazon kvar ba oto.
מצרכי המזון כבר באוטו.
We drink beer or wine during the meal.
Anachnu shotiim beera o ya'een ba'arucha.
אנחנו שותים בירה או יין בארוחה.

Egg – Beitza - ביצה
Eggs - Beitzim – ביצים
Milk – Chalav - חלב
Butter – Chem'ha - חמאה
Cheese - Gvina - גבינה
Bread – Lechem - לחם
Flour – Kemach - קמח
Oil – Shemen - שמן
Baked – Afui - אפוי
Cake – Ooga - עוגה
Beer – Beera - בירה
Wine – Ya'in - יין
Cinnamon – Kinamon - קינמון
Powder – Avka - אבקה
Mustard – Chardal - חרדל

We need to buy flour, eggs, milk, butter, and oil to bake my cake.
Anachnu tzarechim liknot kemach, beitzim, chalav, chem'a, ve shemen kedei lehefot et ha ooga.
אנחנו צריכים לקנות קמח, ביצים, חלב, חמאה ושמן כדי לאפות את העוגה.

For lunch, we can eat seafood, and pasta for dinner.
Le aruchat ha tzohoraiim nochal le'echol peirot yam ve pasta leiaruchat a'erev.
לארוחת הצהריים נוכל לאכול פירות ים ופסטה לארוחת ערב.

I usually eat bread with a slice of cheese for breakfast.
Bederech klal ani ochel prusat lechem iim gvina le aruchat boker.
בדרך כלל אני אוכל פרוסת לחם עם גבינה לארוחת בוקר.

I like ketchup and mustard on my hotdog.
Ani ohev/ohevet ketshop ve chardal al ha nak'nik'iya sheli.
אני אוהב\אוהבת קטשוף וחרדל על הנקניקיה שלי.

The rolls are covered with cinnamon.
Ha lach'mani'yot mechoo'sot (covered) bae kinnamon.
הלחמניות מכוסות בקינמון.

Menu – Tafrit - תפריט
Beef – Bakar - בקר
Lamb – Keves - כבש
Pork – Chazir - חזיר
Steak - Stek – סטייק
Steak - Omtzat basar אומצת בשר
Hamburger - Hamburger המבורגר
Hamburger - Ktzitza קציצה
Water – Ma'iim - מים
Salad – Salat - סלט
Soup – Marak - מרק
Appetizer – Mana rishona – מנה ראשונה
Entrée – Mana eekarit – מנה עיקרית

Do you have a menu in English?
Yesh lecha/lach tafriit bae anglit?
?יש לְךָ\לָךְ תפריט באנגלית

Which is preferable, the fried fish or the grilled lamb?
Ma adiif, ha dag ha metugan o ha keves ba greel?
?מה עדיף, הדג המטוגן או הכבש בגריל

I want to order a cup of water, a soup for my appetizer, and pizza for my entrée.
Ani rotzei/rotza lahazmin cos maiim, marak la mana rishona, ve pizza ke mana eekarit.
.אני רוֹצֶה\רוֹצָה להזמין כוס מים, מרק למנה ראשונה ופיצה כמנה עיקרית

I want to order a steak for myself, a hamburger for my son, and ice cream for my wife.
Ani rotzei lahazmin stek bishvili, hamburger le bni, ve glida le ishti.
.אני רוצה להזמין סטייק בשבילי, המבורגר לפני וגלידה לאישתי

What type of dessert is included with my coffee?
Eizei sugg shel kinuach kalool im ha kafae sheli?
?איזה סוג של קינוח כלול עם הקפה שלי

Cooked – Mevushal - מבושל
Boiled - Mevushal - מבושל
Fried – Metugan - מטוגן
Broiled - Afoo'ee - אפוי
Grilled – Tzalouy - צלוי
Raw - Naa - נא
Raw - Lo mevushal – לא מבושל
Dessert – Kinuach - קינוח
Ice cream - Glida - גלידה
Coffee – Kafé - קפה
Tea – Te'ee - תה
Olive oil – Shemen Zait – שמן זית
Fish – Dag - דג
Juice – Mitz - מיץ
Honey – Dvash - דבש
Sugar – Sucar - סוכר

Can I order a salad with a hard boiled egg and olive oil on the side?
Haiim ochal lahazmiin salat iim beitza kasha ve shemen zait ba tsad?
האם אוכל להזמין סלט עם ביצה קשה ושמן זית בצד.

Is the piece of fish in the sushi cooked or raw?
Hayiim ha chatichat (piece) daag ba sushi naa o mevushal?
האם החתיכות דג בסושי נא או מבושל?

I want to order a fruit juice instead of a soda.
Ani rotzei/rotza lahazmin mitz peirot bimkom soda.
אני רוֹצָה\רוֹצֶה להזמין מיץ פירות במקום סודה.

I want to order tea with a teaspoon of honey instead of sugar.
Ani rotzei/rotza lahazmin tae'ee iim kapit dvash bimkom sucar.
אני רוֹצָה\רוֹצֶה להזמין תה עם כפית דבש במקום סוכר.

The tip is 15% at this restaurant.
Ha tesher (tip) hu chamisha-asar achuz (percent) ba misa'da hazot.
התשר הוא חמישה-עשר אחוז במסעדה הזאת.

Vegetarian – Tzimchoni - צמחוני
Vegan – Ti'vo'ni - טבעוני
Dairy – Chalavi - חלבי
Dairy products - Mutzarei chalav – מוצרי חלב
Salt – Melach - מלח
Pepper – Pilpel - פלפל
Spicy - Charif - חריף
Flavor - Ta'am - טעם
Spices – Tavlinim - תבלינים
Nuts – Egoziim - אגוזים
Peanuts – Botniim - בוטנים

I don't eat meat because I am a vegetarian.
Ani lo ochel/ochelet basar ki ani tzimchoni.
אני לא אוכל\אוכלת בשר כי אני צימחוני.

My brother won't eat dairy products because he is a vegan.
Achi lo ochel motzarei chalav ki hu ti'vo'ni.
אחי לא אוכל מוצרי חלב כי הוא טבעוני.

Food tastes much better with salt, pepper, and other spices.
Ha ochel ta'iim yoter ba melach, pilpel, ve tavliniim acheriim.
האוכל טעים יותר במלח, פלפל ותבלינים אחרים.

The only things I have in my freezer are popsicles.
Ha davar ha yechid shae yesh li ba mikp'a'ha hem karchoniim.
הדבר היחיד שיש לי במקפיא הם קרחונים.

No chocolate, candy, or whipped cream until after dinner.
Ein shokolad, sucaryot, ve katzefet ad achrei aruchat ha erev.
אין שוקולד, סוכריות וקפה אחרי ארוחת ערב.

I want to try a sample of that piece of cheese.
Ani rotzei/rotza lenasot tehima (sample) mi chatichat ha gvina ha zot.
אני רוֹצֶה\רוֹצָה לנסות טעימה מחתיכת הגבינה הזאת.

I have allergies to nuts and peanuts.
Yesh li allerg'ya le egoziim ve le botniim.
יש לי אלרגיה לאגוזים ולבוטנים.

Sauce – Rotev - רוטב
Sandwich – Karich - כריך
Mayonnaise - Mayo'nez - מיונז
Rice – Orez - אורז
Fries – Tships – צ'יפס
Soy – Soya - סויה
Jelly – Riba - ריבה
Chocolate - Chocolat - שוקולד
Cookie - Oo'gui'ya - עוגיה
A candy – Sucarya - סוכריה
Whipped cream – Katzefet - קצפת
Popsicle - Karchon - קרחון
Popsicle - Artik - ארטיק
Frozen – Kafu - קפוא
Thawed – Mufshar - מופשר

This sauce is delicious.
Ha rotev ha'ze mehaneg (delicious) me'od.
הרוטב הזה מענג מאוד.

Why do you always put mayonnaise on your sandwich?
Lama ata/att tamiid saam/saama mayones al ha karich shelcha/shelach.
למה אתה\את תמיד שם\שמה מיונז על הכריך שלך\שלך?

The food is still frozen so we need to wait for it to thaw.
Ha ochel ada'een kafoo'ii ve anachnu tzreichim/treichot lechakot shae'hu yafshir.
האוכל עדיין קפוא ואנחנו צריכים\צריכות לחכות שהוא יפשיר.

Please bring me a bowl of cereal and a slice of toasted bread with jelly.
Bevakasha tavi li ke'arat dganim ve proosat (slice) tost bae riba.
בבקשה תביא לי קערת דגנים ופרוסת טוסט בריבה.

It's healthier to eat rice than fries.
Bari yoter le'echol orez me'asher tships.
בריא יותר לאכול אורז מאשר צ'יפס.

VEGETABLES – YERAKOT - ירקות

Tomato – Agvanya - עגבניה
Carrot – Gezer - גזר
Lettuce – Chasa - חסה
Radish - Tzon'nit - צנונית
Beet - Selek adom – סלק אדום
Chard - Selek lavan – סלק לבן
Eggplant – Chatzil - חציל
Bell Pepper – Pilpel matok - פלפל מתוק
Bell Pepper – gamba – גמבה
Hot pepper – Pilpel charif – פילפל חריף

Grilled vegetables or steamed vegetables are popular side dishes at restaurants.
Yerakot bagrill ve yerakot mehudim hem tosafot me'od mevookashot ba misadot.
ירקות בגריל וירקות מאודים הם תוספות מאוד מבוקשות במסעדות.

There are carrots, bell peppers, lettuce, and radishes in my salad.
Yesh gezer, pilpelim, chasa, ve tznoniyot basalat sheli.
יש גזר, פלפלים, חסה וצנוניות בסלט שלי.

It's not hard to grow tomatoes.
Ze lo kashei legadel agvanyot.
זה לא קשה לגדל עגבניות.

Eggplant can be cooked or fried.
Nitan levashel o letagen chatzil.
ניתן לבשל או לטגן חציל.

I like beets in my salad.
Ani ohev/ohevet selek basalat sheli.
אני אוהב\אוהבת סלק בסלט שלי.

I don't like to eat hot peppers.
Ani lo ohev/ohevet lehechol pilpeliim chariifiim.
אני לא אוהב\אוהבת לאכול פלפלים חריפים.

Celery – Karpas - קרפס
Spinach – Tered - תרד
Cabbage – Kroov - כרוב
Cauliflower – Kroovit - כרובית
Beans – Shae'oo'iit - שעועית
Corn – Tiras - תירס
Garlic – Shoom - שום
Onion – Batsal - בצל
Artichoke – Charshoof - חרשף
Grilled vegetables – Yerakot tzlooyim – ירקות צלויים
Steamed vegetables – Yerakot me'udim – ירוק מאודים

Celery and spinach have natural vitamins.
La karpas ve la tered yesh vitaminim tivi'yim.
לקרפס ולתרד יש ויטמינים טבעיים.

Fried cauliflower tastes better than fried cabbage.
Kroovit metugenet yoter tehima mi kroov metugan.
כרובית מטוגנת יותר טעימה מכרוב מטוגן.

Rice and beans are my favorite side dish.
Orez ve shae'oo'iit em hatosafot ha ha adifot alai.
אורז ושעועית הם התוספות העדיפות עליי.

I like butter on corn.
Ani ohev chemha al ha tee'ras.
אני אוהב חמאה על התירס.

Garlic is an important ingredient in many cuisines.
Shoom hu markiiv chashoov bae ma'achalim rabim.
שום הוא מרכיב חשוב במאכלים רבים.

Where is the onion powder?
Eifo avkaat batsal?
איפה אבקת בצל?

An artichoke is difficult to peel.
Charshoofim hem kashim lekiloof.
חרשופים הם קשים לקילוף.

Cucumber – Malafefon - מלפפון
Lentil – Adashim - עדשים
Peas – Afarsekim - אפרסקים
Green onion – Baz'al Yarok – בצל ירוק
Herbs – Aasvei Tibul – עשבי טיבול
Parsley – Petruzilia - פטרוזיליה
Cilantro – Cusbara - כוסברה
Basil – Bazilikum - בזיליקום
Dill – Shamir - שמיר
Mint – Menta - מנטה

I want to order lentil soup.
Ani roze lehazmin marak adashim
אני רוצה להזמין מרק עדשים.

Please put the green onion in the refrigerator.
Bevakasha sim et ha bazal ha yarok ba mekarer.
בבקשה שים את הבצל הירוק במקרר.

The most common kitchen herbs are basil, cilantro, dill, parsley, and mint.
Tavlinei ha mitbah ha nefoz'im be yoter hem bazilikum, cusbara, shamir, petruzilia ve menta.
תבליני המטבח הנפוצים ביותר הם בזיליקום, כוסברה, שמיר, פטרוזיליה ומנטה.

Some of the most common vegetables for tempura are sweet potatoes and mushrooms.
Helek me ha yerakot ha nefoz'im be yoter la tampura hem batata ve pitriot.
חלק מהירקות הנפוצים ביותר לטמפורה הם בטטה ופטריות.

I want to order vegetarian sushi with asparagus and cucumber, along with a side of seaweed salad.
Ani roze lehazmin sushi tz'imhoni aim esparagos ve malafefon, beyahad aim tosefet shel salat az'ot.
אני רוצה להזמין סושי צימחוני עם אספרגוס ומלפפון, ביחד עם תוספת של סלט אצות.

Potatoes – Tapuah Adama – תפוי אדמה
Sweet Potato – Batata - בטטה
Mushroom – Pitriot - פטריות
Asparagus – Espargos - אספרגוס
Seaweed salad – Salat Az'ot – סלט אצות
Pumpkin – Dla'at – דלעת
Squash – Kishoo - קישוא
Zucchini – zucini – זוקיני
Chick peas – Gargirei Humos – גרגירי חומוס
Vegetable garden – Ginat yerakot – גינת ירקות

The potatoes in the field are ready to harvest.
Ha tapuhei adama ba sade muhanim le kz'ira.
.התפוחי אדמה בשדה מוכנים לקצירה
Chickpeas are the main ingredient to make hummus.
Gargirei humus hem ha markiv ha ikari le haha'nat ha humus.
.גרגירי החומוס הם המרכיב העיקרי להכנת החומוס
Zucchini and squash are from the same family of vegetables.
Zucini ve Kishoo hem me aoto mishpacha shel yerakot.
.קישוא וירקות הם מאותו משפחה של ירקות
Pickled ginger is extremely healthy for you.
Ginger kavush hu meod bar'ee havurha.
.ג'ינג'ר כבוש הוא מאוד בריא עבורך
The tomatoes are fresh but the cucumbers are rotten.
Ha agvaniot trioot aval ha malafefonim rekuvim.
.העגבניות טריות אבל המלפפונים רקובים
I enjoy eating pumpkin seeds as a snack.
Ani nehene lehehol zire'ei dla'at ke hatif.
.אני נהנה לאכול זרעי דלעת כחטיף
I need to water my vegetable garden.
Ani zarih lehashkot et ginat ha yerakot sheli.
.אני צריך להשקות את גינת הירקות שלי
I have an olive grove in my backyard.
Yesh li mata zaitim ba guina sheli.
.יש לי מטע זייתים בגינה שלי

FRUITS - PEIROT - פירות

Apple – Tapuach - תפוח
Orange – Tapuz - תפוז
Grapefruit – Eshkoliit - אשכולית
Peach – Afarsek - אפרסק
Tropical fruit - Peirot tropee'im – פירות טרופים
Papaya – Papaya - פפאיה
Coconut – Cocoos - קוקוס
Cherry – Duvdevan - דובדבן
Grapes – Anaviim - ענבים
Olive – Zait - זית
Grove - Mat'a - מטע

I add either lemon juice or lime juice to my salad.
Ani mohsiif mitz limon o mitz lime la salat sheli.
.אני מוסיף מיץ לימון או מיץ ליים לסלט שלי

Can I add raisins to the apple pie?
Hayiim ani yachol/yechola lehosiif tzimokiim la-oogat ha tapuchiim?
?האם אני יכול\יכולה להוסיף צימוקים לעוגת התפוחים

Orange juice is a wonderful source of Vitamins.
Mitz tapuziim hu makor nifla shel veetamiin'im.
.מיץ תפוזים הוא מקור נפלא של ויטמינים

Grapefruits are extremely beneficial for your health.
Eshkolyot hen me'od me'odafiim (beneficial) la briyut.
.אשכוליות הן מאוד מעודפים לבריאות

I have a peach tree in my front yard
Yesh li etz afarsek ba guina sheli.
.יש לי עץ אפרסק בגינה שלי

I bought papayas and coconuts at the supermarket to prepare a fruit salad.
Kaniti papayot ve cocoos ba super keidei lahachiin salat peirot.
.קניתי פפאיות וקוקוס בסופר כדי להכין סלט פירות

I want to travel to Japan to see the famous cherry blossom.
Ani rotze/rotza linsoha le yapan lir'ott et prichat (blossom) ha duvdevaniim ha mefursemet (famous).
.אני רוצֶה\רוֹצָה לנסוע ליפן לראות את פריחת הדובדבנים המפורסמת

I need to pick the grapes to make the wine.
Ani tzarich/tzreicha liktof anaviim kedei lahachiin et ha yaiin.
.אני צריך\צריכה לקטוף ענבים כדי להכין את היין

Banana – Banana - בננה
Raisins – Tzimookiim - צימוקים
Prune - Shezif meyubash – שזיף מיובש
Dates – Tmarim - תמרים
Fig - Te'ena - תאנה
Fruit salad - Salat peirot – סלט פירות
Dried fruit - Paerot meyoobashiim – פירות מיובשים
Apricot - Mish mesh - מישמש
Pear – Agas - אגס
Avocado – Avocado - אבוקדו
Ripe – Bashel - בשל
Pomegranate – Rimon - רימון

Bananas are tropical fruits.
Bananot hen peirot tropiim.
בננות הן פירות טרופים.

I want to mix dates and figs in my fruit salad.
Ani rotze/rotza le'arbev tmariimn ve te'en'iim ba salat peirot sheli.
אני רוצֶה\רוצָה לערבב תמרים ותאנים בסלט פירות שלי.

Apricots and prunes are my favorite dried fruits.
Mish meshiim ve shezifiim em ha peirot ha yeveshim ha ahooviim alai.
מישמשים ושזיפים הם הפירות היבשים האהובים עליי.

Pears are delicious.
Agasiim me'od tehimim.
אגסים מאוד טעימים

The avocado isn't ripe yet.
Ha avocado adaiin lo bashel.
האבוקדו עדיין לא בשל.

The green apple is very sour.
Ha tapuach ha yarok me'od chamutz.
התפוח הירוק מאוד חמוץ.

The unripe peach is usually bitter.
Ha afarsek boser bederech-klal mar.
האפרסק בוסר בדרך כלל מר.

Pomegranate juice contains a very high level of antioxidants.
Mitz (juice) rimoniim mechil (contains) rama (level) gvoha (high) me'od shel nogdei-chimtzoon (antioxidants).
מיץ רימונים מכיל רמה גבוה מאוד של נוגדי-חימצון.

Fruit tree - Etz peirot – עץ פירות
Citrus - Prei (fruit) hadar (citrus) – פרי הדר
Lemon – Limon - לימון
Lime – Lime - ליים
Pineapple – Ananas - אננס
Melon - Me'lon - מלון
Watermelon – Avatiach - אבטיח
Strawberry - Toot sadei – תות שדה
Berry - Toot - תות
Blueberry – Ochmaniit - אוכמנית
Raspberry – Petel - פטל
Plum – Sheziif - שזיף

Strawberries grow during the Spring.
Toot'ae'ee sad'ae gdelim bae tkoofat ha-aviv.
.תותי שדה גדלים בתקופת האביב

How much does the watermelon juice cost?
Kama olei mitz ha avatiach?
?כמה עולה מיץ האבטיח

I have a pineapple plant in a pot.
Yesh li tzemach ananas ba atzitz (plant pot).
.יש לי צמח אננס בעציץ

Melons grow on the ground.
Meloniim gdeliim ba adama (ground).
.מלונים גדלים באדמה

I am going to the fruit-tree section of the nursery today to purchase a few citrus trees.
Ani olech la chelkat etzi ha prei ba mashtela (nursery) kedei liknot kama etzei (trees) hadar.
.אני הולך לחלקת עצי הפרי במשתלה כדי לקנות כמה עצי הדר

There are many raspberries growing on the bush.
Yesh arbei prei ha godel al siach (bush) ha petel.
.יש הרבה פרי הגדל על שיח הפטל

Blueberry juice is very sweet.
Mitz ochmaniit me'od matok (sweet).
.מיץ אוכמנית מאוד מתוק

Plums are seasonal fruits.
Shezifiim hem paeirot onatee'yiim (seasonal).
.שזיפים הם פירות עונתיים

SHOPPING – KNIYOT - קניות

Clothes – Bgadiim - בגדים
Clothing store - Chanoot bgadiim – חנות בגדים
For sale – Lemechira - למכירה
Shirt – Chooltza - חולצה
Shoes - Na'ala'iim - נעליים
Sneakers - Na'alei sport נעלי ספורט
Hat – Kova - כובע
Skirt – Chatzaiit - חצאית
Dress – Simlah - שמלה
Pants – Michnasaiim - מכנסיים
Shorts – Michnasaiim ktzariim – מכנסיים קצרים
Suit – Chalifa - חליפה
Vest – Afooda - אפודה
Tie – Aniva - עניבה

There are a lot of clothes for sale today.
Yesh hayom harbei bgadiim le mechira.
יש היום הרבה בגדים למכירה.
Does this hat look good?
Hakova hazei nir'a tov?
הכובע הזה נראה טוב?
I am happy with this shirt and these shoes.
Ani samei'ach/(f)smeicha ba chooltza ve ba na'aliim ha el'ae.
אני שמח\שמחה בחולצה ובנעליים שלי.
She prefers a skirt instead of a dress.
Hee mahadifa chatzahiit al simlah.
אני מעדיפה חצאית על שמלה.
These pants aren't my size.
Ha michnasiim ha elu lo bameeda sheli.
המכנסיים האלו לא במידה שלי.
Where can I find a thrift store? I want to buy a suit, a vest, and a tie.
Eifo oochal limtzo chanut yad shniya? Ani rotze liknot chalifa, afooda, ve aniva.
איפה אוכל למצוא חנות יד שנייה? אני רוצה לקנות חליפה, אפודה ועניבה.

Uniform – Madiim - מדים
Belt – Chagora - חגורה
Socks – Garbaiim - גרביים
Gloves – Kfafot - כפפות
Glasses – Mishkafiim - משקפיים
Sunglasses - Mishkafei shemesh – משקפי שמש
Size – Meeda - מידה
Small – Katan - קטן
Medium – Beinoni - בינוני
Large - Gadol - גדול
Thick - Av'ae - עבה
Thin – Dak - דק
Thrift store - Chanuut yad shni'ya – חנות יד שנייה

There are uniforms for school at the clothing store.
Ba chanut ha bgadiim yesh madiim shel bet ha sefer.
בחנות הבגדים יש מדים של בית הספר.

I forgot my socks, belt, and shorts at your house.
Shachachti et hagarbaiim, chagora, ve ha michnasiim ha ktzariim sheli ba ba'iit shelcha.
שכחתי את הגרביים, חגורה והמכנסיים הקצרים שלי בבית שלך.

These gloves are a size too small. Do you have a medium size?
Ha kfafot ha helu hen ktanot meedai. Yesh lecha meeda bey'noniit?
הכפפות האלו הן קטנות מידי. יש לך מידה בינונית?

Today I don't need my reading glasses. However, I have my sunglasses.
Hayom ani lo tzarich/tzreicha et mishkafei ha kreiya sheli. Aval yesh li et mishkafei ha shemesh sheli.
היום אני לא צריך\צריכה את משקפי הקריאה שלי. אבל יש לי את משקפי השמש שלי.

Jacket - Mae'il katzar – מעיל קצר
Scarf - Tze'hiif - צעיף
Mittens – Kfafot - כפפות
Sleeve – Sharvool - שרוול
Boots (rain, winter) – Magafahiim - מגפיים
Sweater – Sveder - סוודר
Bathing suit - Beigaed yam – בגד ים
Flip flops – Kafkafiim – כפכפים
Tank top - Gufi'ya - גופיה

We are going to the mountain today so don't forget your jacket, mittens, and scarf.
Anachnu olim/olot lahariim hayom az al tishkach/tishkechi et ha mae'hil, ha kfafot, ve ha tzahiff shelcha/shelach
אנחנו עולים\עולות להרים היום אז אל תשכח\תשכחי את המעיל, הכפפות והצעיף שֶׁלְךָ\שֶׁלָךְ.

I have long sleeve shirts and short sleeve shirts.
Yesh li chultza iim sharvool'eem arukiim ve sharvool'eem ktzariim.
יש לי חולצה עם שרוולים ארוכים ושרוולים קצרים.

Boots and sweaters are meant for winter.
Magafiim ve svederiim meyu'adiim (meant for) la choref.
מגפיים וסנדלים מיועדים לחורף.

At the beach, I wear a bathing suit and flip flops.
Bachoff ani lovesh beigaed yam ve no'el (wear shoes) kafkafiim.
בחוף אני לובש בגד ים ונועל כפכפים.

I want to buy a tank top for summer.
Ani rotzei/rotza liknot gufiya la ka'itz.
אני רוֹצָה\רוֹצָה לקנות גופיה לקיץ.

Sandals – Sandaliim - סנדלים
Heels – Akeviim - עקבים
On sale - Mivtz'a mechirot – מבצע מכירות
Expensive – Yakar - יקר
Free - Bae-chinam - בחינם
Discount – Hanacha - הנחה
Cheap – Zoll - זול
Shopping – Kniyot - קניות
Mall – Kanyon - קניון

I can't wear heels on the beach, only sandals.
Ani lo yechola lin'ol akeviim le chof ha yaam, raak sandaliim.
אני לא יכולה לנעול עקבים לחוף הים, רק סנדלים.

What will be on sale tomorrow?
Ma yee'hyae bae mivtz'a mechirot machar?
מה יהיה במבצע מכירות מחר?

This is free.
Ze bechinam.

Even though this cologne and this perfume are discounted, they are still very expensive.
Lahmrot shae ha mei ha kolone ve ha bosem hazei bae hanacha, hem a'daiin me'od yekar'eem.
למרות שהמי הקלן והבושם הזה בהנחה, הם עדיין מאוד יקרים.

These items are very cheap.
Ha mutzar'iim ha elu me'od zoliim.
המוצרים האלו מאוד זולים.

I can go shopping only on weekends.
Ani yachol latzet lekniyot raak bae sofei shavu'ha.
אני יכול לצאת לקניות רק בסופי שבוע.

Is the local mall far?
Haiim ha kenyon ha mekomi rachok?
האם הקניון המקומי רחוק?

Store – Chanoot - חנות
Business hours - Sha'hott avoda – שעות עבודה
Open – Patuach - פתוח
Closed – Sagoor - סגור
Entrance – Knisa - כניסה
Exit – Yetziya - יציאה
Shopping cart - Agalat kniyot – עגלת קניות
Shopping basket - Saall kni'yot – סל קניות
Shopping bag - Sakiit kniyot – שקית קניות
Toy store - Chanut tza'ha'tzu'iim – חנות צעצועים
Toy - Tza'ha'tzu'ha - צעצוע
Book store - Chanut sfariim – חנות ספרים

What are your (plural) business hours?
Ma hen sha'ot ha avoda shelachem?
מה הן שעות העבודה שלכם?
What time does the store open?
Bae eize sha'a niftachat ha chanoot?
באיזה שעה נפתחת החנות?
What times does the store close?
Bae-ei-zo shaha nisgaeret ha chanoot?
באיזו שעה החנות נסגרת?
Where is the entrance?
Eifo ha knissa?
איפה הכניסה?
Where is the exit?
Eifo ha yetzi'ya?
איפה היציאה?
My children want to go to the toy store so they can fill up the shopping cart with toys.
Ha yeladim sheli rotzim lalechet la chanut tzahatzu'im ke'dei lemalae et agalat ha kniyot baetza'ha'tzu'iim.
הילדים שלי רוצים ללכת לחנות צעצועים כדי למלא את עגלת הקניות בצעצועים.

Music store - Chanut le musica – חנות למוזיקה
Jeweler - Tachsheet'ai - תכשיטאי
Jewelry - Tach'sheet - תכשיט
Gold – Zahav - זהב
Silver – Kessef - כסף
Necklace – Machrozet מחרוזת
Necklace – Sharsheret שרשרת
Bracelet – Tzamiid - צמיד
Diamond - Ya'halom - יהלום
Gift – Matana - מתנה
Coin - Matbaei'a - מטבע
Antique - Atikiim – עתיקים
Antique - (f) Atikot - עתיקות
Dealer – Socher - סוחר

I use a large shopping basket at the supermarket.
Ani mishtamesh bae saall kniyot gadol ba supermarket.
אני משתמש בסל קניות גדול בסופרמרקט.
There is a sale at the bookstore right now.
Yesh mivtza bae chanoot ha sfariim hayom.
יש מבצע בחנות הספרים היום.
The jeweler sells gold and silver.
Ha tach'sheet'ai mocher zahav ve kesef.
התכשיטאי מוכר זהב וכסף.
I want to buy a diamond necklace.
Ani rotzei/rotza liknot machrozet yahalomiim.
אני רוֹצֶה\רוֹצָה לקנות מחרוזת יהלומים.
This bracelet and those pair of earrings are gifts for my daughter.
Ha tzamiid hazei ve zoog (pair) ha agilim ha elu hem matanot la bat sheli.
הצמיד הזה וזוג העגילים האלו הם מתנות לבת שלי.
He is an antique coin dealer.
Hu socher matbe'ott atikiim.
הוא סוחר מטבעות עתיקים.

FAMILY – MISHPACHA - משפחה

Mother - Em אם
Mother - Imma – אמא
Father - Av אב
Father - Aba – אבא
Son – Ben - בן
Daughter – Bat - בת
Brother – Ach - אח
Sister – Achot - אחות
Husband - Ba'al - בעל
Wife – Isha - אישה
Parent – Horei - הורה
Parents – Horiim - הורים
Child - Yeled - ילד
Child - (f) yalda - ילדה
Baby – Tinok - תינוק

I have a big family.
Yesh li mishpacha gdola.
.יש לי משפחה גדולה

My brother and sister are here.
Achi ve achoti kan.
.אחי ואחותי כאן

The mother and father want to spend time with their child.
Ha em va ha av rotzim levalot-et-ha-zman (spend time) iim ha yeladiim shelahem.
.האם והאב רוצים לבלות את הזמן עם הילדים שלהם

He wants to bring his son and daughter to the public park.
Hu rotzei lahavi et bno ve beito la gan ha tzibooree (public).
.הוא רוצה להביא את בנו ובתו לגן הציבורי

Hu rotzei lahavi et ha bat shelo ve et ha ben shelo la gan ha tzibooree (public).
.הוא רוצה להביא את הבת שלו ואת הבן שלו לגן הציבורי

Grandfather – Saba - סבא
Grandmother – Savta - סבתא
Grandparents – Sabim - סבים
Grandson – Neched - נכד
Granddaughter – Nechda - נכדה
Grandchildren – Nechadim - נכדים
Nephew – Achyan - אחיין
Niece – Achyanit - אחיין
Cousin - (M) Ben dod – בן דוד
Cousin - (F) bat doda – בת דודה

The grandfather wants to take his grandson to the movie.
Ha saba rotzei lakachat et ha neched shelo laseret.
הסבא רוצה לקחת את הנכד שלו לסרט.
The grandmother wants to give her granddaughter money.
Ha savta rotza latet la nechda shela kesef.
הסבתא רוצה לתת לנכדה שלה כסף.
The grandparents want to spend time with their grandchildren.
Ha sabiim rotzim levalot et hazman iim ha nechadiim.
הסבים רוצים לבלות את הזמן עם הנכדים.
The husband and wife have a new baby.
La ba'al ve la isha yesh tinok chadash.
לבעל ולאישה יש תינוק חדש.
I want to go to the park with my niece and nephew.
Ani rotzei/rotza lalechet la gan ha tzibooree iim ha achyan ve ha achyaniit sheli.
אני רוֹצֶה\רוֹצָה ללכת לגן הציבורי עם האחיין והאחיינית שלי.
My cousin wants to see his children.
Ben ha dod sheli rotzei lir'ott et yeladav.
בן הדוד שלי רוצה לראות את ילדיו.
That man is a good parent.
Ha iish azei hu hor'ae tov.
האיש הזה הוא הורה טוב.

Aunt – Doda - דודה
Uncle – Dodd - דוד
Man - Ish - איש
Woman – Isha - אישה
Stepfather - Aba choreg – אבא חורג
Stepmother - Ima choreg'et – אמא חורגת
Stepbrother - Ach choreg – אבא חורג
Stepsister - Achot chorg'et – אחות חורגת
Stepson - Ben choreg – בן חורג
Stepdaughter - Bat choreget – בת חורגת
In laws – Mechootaniim - מחותנים
Ancestors – Avot - אבות
Family tree - Etz mishpachti – עץ משפחה
Generation – Dor - דור
First born - Ben bechor – בן בכור
First born - (f) Bat bchora – בת בכורה
Only child - Ben yachid - בן יחיד
Only child - (f) Bat yechida – בת יחידה

My aunt and uncle came here for a visit.
Ha dod ve hadoda ba'oo levaker.
הדוד והדודה באו לבקר.
He is their only child.
Hu ha yeled ha yachid shelahem.
הוא הילד היחיד שלהם.
My wife is pregnant with twins.
Ishti beherayon ve yesh la te'omiim.
אישתי בהריון ויש לה תאומים.
He is their eldest son.
Hu ha ben ha yachid shelahem.
הוא הבן היחיד שלהם.
The first-born child usually takes on all the responsibilities.
Ha ben habechor bederchklal lokaei'ach al atzmo et kol ha achrayut (responsibility).
הבן הבכור בדרך כלל לוקח על עצמו את כל האחריות.

Relative - Karov mishpacha – קרוב משפחה
Family member - Ben mishpacha – בן משפחה
Twins - Te'omiim תאומים
Twins - Te'omot תאומות
Pregnant - Behe'rayon - בהריון
Adopted child - Yeled me'oomatz – ילד מאומץ
Orphan – Yatom -יתום
Adult – Mevugar - מבוגר
Neighbor – Shachen - שכן
Neighbor – (f) schaena - שכנה
Friend – Chaver - חבר
Friend – (f) Chavera - חברה
Roommate - Shootaf la dira – שותף לדירה (shootaf as a stand alone word means "partner")

I was able to find all my relatives and ancestors on my family tree.
Hetzlachti limtzo et kol krovei ha mishpacha sheli al ha etz ha mishpachti.
הצלחתי למצוא את כל קרובי המשפחה שלי על העץ המשפחתי.

My parents' generation loved disco music.
Dor ha oriim sheli hohev musicat disco.
דור ההורים שלי אוהב מוזיקת דיסקו.

Their adopted child was an orphan
Yaldam ha me'oomatz haya yatom / ha yeled ha me'oomatz shelahem haya yatom.
ילדם המאומץ היה יתואם \ הילד המאומץ שלהפ היה יתום.

I like my in-laws.
Ani ohev/ohevet et ha mechootaniim sheli.
אני אוהב\אוהבת את המחותנים שלי.

I have a nice neighbor.
Yesh li shachen/schena nechmad/nechmada.
יש לי שכן\שכנה נחמד\נחמדה.

She considers her stepson as her real son.
Hee mach'shiiva (she considers) et bna ha choreg ke-bna ha amiti.
היא מחשיבה את בנה החורג כבנה האמיתי.

She is his stepdaughter.
Hee ha bat ha choreget shelo.
היא הבת החורגת שלו.

HUMAN BODY - GOOF HA AADAM – גוף האדם

Head – Rosh - ראש
Face – Paniim - פנים
Eye - A'iin - עין
Eye - (p) aiin'aeem - עיניים
Ear – Ozen - אוזן
Ear – (p) ozn'yaeem - אוזניים
Nose – Aaf - אף
Mouth – Pae - פה
Lips – Sfatiim – שפתיים

My chin, cheeks, mouth, lips, and eyes are all part of my face.
Ha santer, ha lechayaiim, ha pae, ve ha a'iinaim sheli em koolam chelek mi ha-panim sheli.
הסנטר, הלחיים, הפה והעיניים שלי הם כולם חלק מהפנים שלי.

He has small ears.
Yesh lo ozn'yaeem ktanot. (Although the ending is masc the gender is fem)
יש לו אוזניים קטנות.

I have a cold so therefore my nose, eyes, mouth, and tongue are affected.
Ani metzunan lachen (therefore) ha aaf, a'iinaim, pae, ve ha lashon sheli pgoo'iim.
אני מצונן לכן האף, עיניים, פה והלשון שלי פגועים.

The five senses are sight, touch, taste, smell, and hearing.
Chameshet ha chushiim (senses) hem rey'ha, neg'ee'ya, ta'am, raei'ach, ve shmia'a.
חמשת החושים הם ראייה, נגיעה, טעם, ריח ושמיעה.

I am washing my face right now.
Ani rochetz et panaii achshav.
אני רוחץ את פניי עכשיו.

I have a headache
Yesh li ke'ev rosh.
יש לי כאב ראש.

My eyebrows are too long.
Hagabot sheli me'od harukot.
הגבות שלי מאוד ארוכות.

Tongue – Lashon - לשון
Cheek – Lechi - לחי
Chin – Santer - סנטר
Neck – Tzavar - צוואר
Throat – Garon - גרון
Forehead – Metzach - מצח
Skin – Orr - עור
Eyebrow – Gaba - גבה
Eyelashes – Rissim - ריסים
Hair - Say'ar - שיער
Beard – Zakan - זקן
Mustache – Safam - שפם
Tooth – Shen - שן
Tooth – (p) sheen'aeem - שיניים

He must shave his beard and mustache.
Hu tzarich le'galei'ach et ha zakan ve et ha safam shelo.
הוא צריך לגלח את הזקן ואת השפם שלו.
I brush my teeth every morning.
Ani metzachtzeiach et ha shinaiim sheli kol boker.
אני מצחצח את השיניים שלי כל בוקר.
She puts makeup on her cheeks and a lot of lipstick on her lips.
Hee me'aperet (puts makeup) et ha lechayaiim shela ve sama arbei odem ba sfata'yeem.
היא מאפרת את הלחיים שלה ושמה הרבה אודם בשפתיים.
Her hair covered her forehead.
Ha say'ar shela keesa et hametzach shela.
השיער שלה כיסה את המצח שלה.
She has a long neck.
Yesh la tzavar aroch.
יש לה צוואר ארוך.
I have a sore throat.
Yesh li daleket (infection) ba garon.
יש לי דלקת בגרון.
I have beautiful skin.
Yesh lee orr yaf'ae.
יש לי עור יפה.

Shoulder – Katef - כתף
Chest - Cha'zei - חזה
Arm - Zro'aa - זרוע
Hand - Yad - יד
Palm (of hand) - Kaf ha yad – כף היד
Elbow – Marpek - מרפק
Wrist - Mifrak ha yad – מפרק היד
Finger – Etzba - אצבע
Thumb – Agudal - אגודל
Belly – Beten - בטן
Stomach – Keiva - קיבה
Intestines - Mei'a'aiim - מעיים
Brain - Mo'ach
Heart - Lev
Kidneys - Klayot
Lungs - Rey'ott - ריאות
Liver – Kaved - כבד

He has a problem with his stomach.
Yesh lo bahayot iim ha keiva shelo.
.יש לו בעיות עם הקיבה שלו

The brain, heart, kidneys, lungs, and liver are internal organs.
Ha mo'ach, lev, klayot, rey'ott, ve ha kaved em avariim-pnim'iim (internal organs).
.המוח, לב, כליות, ריאות והכבד הם איברים פנימיים

His chest and shoulders are very muscular.
Ha chazei ve haktefaiim shelo hem me'od shrir'iim (muscular).
.החזה והכתפיים שלו הם מאוד שריריים

I need to strengthen my arms and legs.
Ani tzarich lechazek et yadai ve raglai / et ha yadaiim ve et ha raglaiim sheli.
.אני צריך לחזק את ידיי ורגליי \ את הידיים והרגליים שלי

I accidentally hit his wrist with my elbow.
Bae-mikrei (accidentally) pagaa'tee ba mifrak ha yad shelo iim ha marpek sheli.
.במקרה פגעתי במפרק היד שלו עם המרפק שלי

Leg - Reg'el - רגל
Ankle – Karsool - קרסול
Foot – Regel - רגל
Palm (of foot) - Kaf ha reg'el – כף הרגל
Toe – Bohen - בוהן
Nail – Tziporen - ציפורן
Joint – Mifrak - מפרק
Muscle – Shrir - שריר
Back – Gav - גב
Spine - Amud shidra – עמוד שדרה
Skeleton – Sheled - שלד
Bone – Etzem - עצם
Ribs - Tzla'ot - צלעות
Skull – Golgolet - גולגולת
Vein – Vreed - וריד
Artery - Orek - עורק

I have pain in every part of my body especially in my hand, ankle, and back.
Yesh li ke'eviim bekol chelkei goofi bimyuchad ba yad, karsool, ve bagav sheli.
יש לי כאבים בכל חלקי גופי במיוחד ביד, קרסול ובגב שלי.

I want to cut my nails.
Ani rotzei lekatzetz et hatzipornaiim sheli.
אני רוצה לכצץ את הציפורניים שלי.

I need a new bandage for my thumb.
Ani tzarich retiya chadasha beshvil ha agudal sheli.
אני צריך רטייה חדשה בשביל האגודל שלי.

I have a cast on my foot because of a broken bone.
Yesh li geves (cast) ba regel biglal ha etzem ha shvora.
יש לי גבס ברגל בגלל העצם השבורה.

I have muscles and joint pain today.
Yesh li ke'evim ba shririm hoo ba mifrakiim sheli. (Before *ba* the "and" is *hoo*.)
יש לי כאבים בשרירים ובמפרקים שלי.

The spine is the main part of the body.
Amud ha shidra hu ha chelek ha ikarei (main) ba goof.
עמוד השדרה הוא החלק העיקרי בגוף.

HEALTH AND MEDICAL
BRI'OOT VE RE'FOO'HA - בריאות ורפואה

Disease – Machala - מחלה
Bacteria - Bakteria - בקטריה
Germ - Chay'dak – חיידק
Sick – Cholei - חולה
Clinic - Mirpa'aa - מרפאה
Clinic - Clinika – קליניקה
Headache - Ke'ev rosh – כאב ראש
Earache - Ke'ev oznaiim – כאב אוזניים
Pharmacy - Beit merkachat – בית מרקחת
Prescription – Mirsham - מרשם
Symptoms – Tasminim - תסמינים
Nausea – Bchila - בחילה
Stomachache - Ke'ev beten – כאב בטן
Allergy - Alerg'ya - אלרגיה

Are you in good health?
A'iim ata/att bebri'yoot tova?
האם אתה\את בבריאות טובה?

These bacteria caused this disease.
Ha chaidakiim ha helu garmu la machala hazut.
החיידקים האלו גרמו למחלה הזאת.

He is very sick.
Hu me'od cholei.
הוא מאוד חולה.

I have a headache so I must go to the pharmacy to refill my prescription.
Yesh li ke'ev rosh az alai lalechet la beit merkachat kedei lemalae mechadash et ha mirsham sheli.
יש לי כאב ראש אז עליי ללכת לבית מרקחת כדי למלא מחדש את המרשם שלי.

The main symptoms of food poisoning are nausea and stomach ache.
Ha simptomim ha yekariim shel ar'alat mazon em bchila ve ke'hev beten.
הסימפטומים עיקריים של הרעלת מזון הם בחילה וכאב בטן.

Penicillin – Penitzilin - פניצילין
Antibiotic – Antibiotica - אנטיביוטיקה
Sore throat - Ke'ev garon – כאב גרון
Fever - Chom - חום
Flu – Shapaat - שפעת
Cough - Shi'ool - שיעול
To cough - Lehishta'el - להשתעל
Infection – Daleket - דלקת
Injury - Ptzi'ya - פציעה
Scar – Tzaleket - צלקת
Ache / pain - Ke'ev - כאב
Intensive care - Tipul nimratz – טיפול נמרץ
Bandaid - Retiya - רטייה
Bandaid - Plaster - פלסטר
Bandage – Tachboshet - תחבושת

I have an allergy to penicillin, so I need another antibiotic.
Yesh li alergia le penitzilin as ani tzarich/tzreicha antibiotica acheret.
יש לי אלרגיה לפניצילין אז אני צריך\צריכה אנטיביוטיקה אחרת.
What do I need to treat an earache?
Ma ani tzarich/tzreicha letapel bae ke'ev oznaiim.
מה אני צריך\צריכה לטפל בכאב אוזניים.
I need to go to the clinic for my fever and sore throat.
Ani tzarich/tzreicha lalechet la mirpa'a biglal ha chom ve ke'ev ha garon.
אני צריך\צריכה ללכת למרפאה בגלל החום וכאב הגרון.
The bandage won't help your infection.
Ha tachboshet lo tahazor la daleket shelcha/shelach.
התחבושת לא תעזור לדלקת שֶׁלְךָ\שֶׁלָּךְ.
I have a serious injury so I must go to intensive care.
Yesh li ptziya kasha ve lachen ala'yee lalechet le tipul nimratz.
יש לי פציעה קשה ולכן עליי ללכת לטיפול נמרץ.
I have muscle and joint pains today.
Hayom yesh li ke'e'vei shririm ve mifrakim.
היום יש לי כאבי שרירים ומפרקים.

Hospital - Beit cholim – בית חולים
Doctor – Rofei - רופא
Nurse – Achot - אחות
Family Doctor - Rofei mishpacha – רופא משפחה
Pediatrician - Rofei yeladiim – רופא ילדים
Medication - Troofa - תרופה
Pills - Kaduriim כדורים
Pills - Gloo'lot גלולות
Heartburn – Tzarevet - צרבת
Paramedic - Chovesh חובש
Paramedic - Paramedic פרמדיק
Emergency room - Chadar mi'yoon – חדר מיון
Patient – Cholei – חוֹלֶה
Patient – (f) Chola - חוֹלָה
Surgery - Ni'tuach - ניתוח
Surgeon - Mena'tei'ach - מנתח
Face mask - Masechat pan'eem – מסיכת פנים
Anesthesia – Hardama - הרדמה
Local anesthesia - Hardama mekomit – הרדמה מקומית
General anesthesia - Hardama klalit – הרדמה כללית

Where is the closest hospital?
Eifo beit ha choliim ha karov bae yoter?
איפה בית החולים הקרוב ביותר?
Usually we see the nurse before the doctor.
Bederich'klal anu ro'eiim et ha achot lifnei ha rofei.
בדרך כלל אנו רואים את האחות לפני הרופא.
The paramedics can take her to the emergency room but she doesn't have health insurance.
Ha chovshiim yecholim lakachat ota la chadar mi'yuun aval ein la bituach re'foo'ee.
החובשים יכולים לקחת אותה לחדר מיון אבל אין לה ביטוח רפואי.
The doctor treated the patient.
Ha rofei tipel ba cholei.
הרופא טיפל בחולה.
He needs knee surgery today.
Hu tzarich nitoo'ach ba ber'ech.
הוא צריך ניתוח בברך.

Wheelchair - Kisei galgaliim – כיסא גלגלים
Cane - Mishe'enet - משענת
Walker – Halichon - הליכון
Stretcher – Aloonka - אלונקה
Health insurance - Bituach re'foo'ee – ביטוח רפואי
Dialysis - Dai'aliza - דיאליזה
Insulin - Insoolin – אינסולין
Diabetes – Sakeret - סכרת
Temperature – Chom - חום
Thermometer – Madchom – מד חום
A shot – Zrika - זריקה
Needle – Machat - מחט
Syringe – Mazrek - מזרק
In need of - (M) Zakook - זקוק
In need of - (F) Zkooka - זקוקה

The surgeon needs to administer general anesthesia in order to operate on the patient.
Ha menatei'ach tzarich lehazrik hardama klalit kedi le'natei'ach et ha cholei.
.המנתח צריך להזריק הרדמה כללית כדי לנתח את החולה

Does the patient need a wheelchair or a stretcher?
Hayiim ha cholei zakook lekisei galgaliim o aloonka?
?האם החולה זקוק לכיסא גלגלים או אלונקה

I have to take medicine every day.
Ani tzarich/tzreicha lakachat troofa kol yom.
.אני צריך\צריכה לקחת תרופה כל יום

Do you have any pills for heartburn?
Yesh lecha/lach kadoorim letzarevet?
.יש לְךָ\לָךְ כדורים לצרבת

Where is the closest dialysis center?
Eifo merkaz ha dai'aliza ha karov beyoter?
?איפה מרכז הדיאליזה הקרוב ביותר

The doctor didn't prescribe insulin for my diabetes.
Ha rofei lo rasham li insoolin bishvil ha sakeret.
.הרופא לו רשם לי אינסולין בשביל הסכרת

I need a thermometer to take my temperature.
Ani tzarich madchom kedei limdod (to measure) et ha chom sheli.
.אני צריך מדחום כדי למדוד את החום שלי

Stroke - Ee'roo'ha mochi – אירוע מוחי
Blood – Daam - דם
Blood pressure - Lachatz daam – לחץ דם
Heart attack - Etkef lev – התקף לב
Cancer – Sartan - סרטן
Chemotherapy - Chemotrap'ya - כימותרפיה
Help – Ezra - עזרה
Germs – Chaidakiim - חיידקים
Virus - Viroos וירוס/ nag'eef – נגיף
Vaccine – Chisun - חיסון
A cure – Ripui - ריפוי
To cure - Lerap'ae - לרפא
Cholesterol – Colestrol - כולסטרול
Nutrition - Tzu'na - תזונה
Diet - Dee'eta - דיאטה
Blind – Iver - עיוור
Deaf – Cheresh - חרש
Mute - Ei'lem - אילם

A stroke is caused by a lack of blood flow to the brain.
Ee'roo'ha mochi nigram mi choser zrimat daam la mo'ach
אירוע מוחי נגרם מחוסר זרימת דם למוח.
These are the symptoms of a heart attack.
Elei ha tismooniim shel etkef lev.
אלה התסמונים של התקף לב.
Chemotherapy is for treating cancer.
Ha chemotrap'ya hee letipul bae sartan.
הכימותרפיה היא לטיפול בסרטן.
Proper nutrition is very important and you must avoid foods that are high in cholesterol.
Tzu'na nechona me'od chashoova ve aleichem le'himana mi ma'achaliim atirei kolestrol.
תזונה נכונה מאוד חשובה ועליכם להימנע ממאכלים עתירי כולסטרול.
I am starting my diet today.
Ani matchil/matchila et ha dieta sheli hayom.
אני מתחיל\מתחילה את הדיאטה שלי היום.

Young - Tza'eer - צעיר, **Young** - (f) Tza'eera - צעירה
Elderly – Mevoogar - מבוגר,
Elderly – (f) Mevoogeret - מבוגרת
Fat – Shooman - שומן
Fat (person) – Shamen - שָמֵן / **Fat** (person) – (f) Shmena - שמנה
Skinny (person) – Razei - רָזֶה,
Skinny (person) – (f) Ra'za - רָזָה
Nursing home - Beit avot – בית אבות
Assisted living - Dioor moogan – דיור מוגן
Disability, handicap – Nechut - נכות
Paralysis - Shee'took - שיתוק
Depression - Dika'honn - דיכאון
Anxiety – Charada - חרדה
X-ray - Tziloom roentgen – צילום רנטגן
Dentist - Rofei shina'iim – רופא שיניים
Tooth cavity - Nekev bashen – נקב בשן
Tooth paste - Mishchat shina'iim – משחת שיניים
Tooth brush - Mivreshet shina'iim – מברשת שיניים

There is no cure for this virus, only a vaccine.
Ein ripui la nag'eef hazei, yesh rak chisun.
.אין ריפוי לנגיף הזה, יש רק חיסון

The nursing home is open 365 days a year.
Beit ha'avot patuach kol yom ba shana.
.בית אבות פתוח כל יום בשנה

I don't like suffering from depression and anxiety.
Ani lo ohev/ohevet lisbol mi dikahon ve charada.
.אני לא אוהב\אוהבת לסבול מדיכאון וחרדה

Soap and water kill germs.
Sabon ve maiim org'iim chaydakiim.
.סבון ומים הורגים חיידקים

The dentist took X-rays of my teeth to check for cavities.
Rofei ha shinaiim lakach tziloom rentgen shel ha shinaiim sheli.
.רופא השיניים לקח צילום רנטגן של השיניים שלי

In the morning I put tooth paste on my toothrbush.
Baboker ani moreiach mishcha al ha mivreshet lifnei kol davar.
.בבוקר אני מורח משחה על המברשת לפני כל דבר

EMERGENCY & DISASTERS
CHEROOM VE ASONOT – חירום ואסונות

Help – Ezra - עזרה
Fire – Srefa - שריפה
Ambulance – Ambulans - אמבולנס
First aid - Ezra rishona – עזרה ראשונה
CPR - Achi'ya / pe'ulat achi'ya'a – החייאה \ פעולת החייאה
Emergency number - Mispar cheroom – מספר חירום
Accident - Te'una - תאונה
Car crash - Te'unat drachiim – תאונת דרכים
Death – Mavet - מוות
Deadly – Katlani - קטלני
Fatality - Har'oog - הרוג
Lightly wounded - Patzu'a kaal – פצוע קל
Moderately wounded - Patzu'a beinoni – פצוע בינוני
Seriously wounded - Patzu'a kashei – פצוע קשה

There is a fire. I need to call for help.
Yesh srefa. Ani tzarich lehitkasher le hatzala.
יש שריפה. אני צריך להתקשר להצלה.
I need to call an ambulance.
Ani tzarich/tzreicha lehazmin (to call for) ambulans.
אני צריך\צריכה להזמין אמבולנס.
That accident was bad.
Ha te'una hayta kasha.
התאונה הייתה קשה.
The thief wants to steal my money.
Haganav rotzei lignov et ha kesef sheli.
הגנב רוצה לגנוב את הכסף שלי.
The car crash was fatal, there were two deaths, and four suffered serious injuries.
Te'unat drachiim hayta katlanit, haiyu shnei haroog'iim ve aarb'a ptzuiim kashei.
תאונת דרכים הייתה קטלנית, היו שני הרוגים וארבעה פצועים.

Fire truck - Kaba'iit - כבאית
Siren - Tzfira, sirena – סירנה, צפירה
Fire extinguisher - Mataf kiboo'yee esh – מטף כיבוי אש
Police – Mishtara - משטרה
Police station - Tachanat mishtara – תחנת משטרה
Robbery - Shod שוד, gnei'va – גניבה
Thief - Ganav - גנב
Murderer - Rotzei'ach - רוצח

One was moderately wounded and two were lightly wounded.
Eichad haya patzua benoni ve shnaiim hayu ptzuiim kaal.
אחד היה פצוע בינוני ושניים היו פצועים קל.

CPR is a first step of first-aid.
Achi'ya'a hu tzaad rishon bae ezra rishona.
החייאה הוא צעד ראשון בעזרה ראשונה.

Please provide me with the emergency number.
Bevakasha ten li et mispar ha telefon shel merkaz cheroom.
בבקשה תן לי את מספר הטלפון של מרכז החירום.

The police are on their way.
Ha mishtara ba dereich.
המשטרה בדרך.

I must call the police station to report a robbery.
Alai lehitkasher la mishtara kedei ledaveiach shodd.
עליי להתקשר למשטרה כדי לדווח שוד.

The siren of the fire truck is very loud.
Tzfirat ha kabaiit ro'eshet me'od.
צפירת הקיבוץ רועשת מאוד.

Where is the fire extinguisher?
Eifo ha mataf kibui ha esh?
איפה המטף כיבוי האש?

There is a fire. I must call for help.
Yesh sreifa. Alai lehitkasher le hatzala.
יש שריפה. עליי להתקשר לעזרה.

Fire hydrant - Berez kibuui – ברז כיבוי
Fireman - Kabaiim כבאים
Fireman - Mecabei esh - מכבי אש
Emergency situation - Matzav cheiroom – מצב חירום
Explosion – Hitpotzetzut - התפוצצות
Rescue – Hatzala - הצלה
Natural disaster - Ason teva – אסון טבע
Destruction – Heres - הרס
Damage – Nezek - נזק
Hurricane – Hurican - הוריקן
Tornado – Tornado - טורנדו
Flood - Mabool מבול
Flood - Sheetafon – שיטפון
Disaster – Asonn - אסון
Disaster area - Ezor ha asonn – איזור האסון
Mandatory – Chova - חובה
Evacuation – Pinui - פינוי

It's prohibited to park by the fire hydrant in case of a fire.
Asoor (prohibited) lachanot letzad mitkan ha esh lemikrei sreifa.
אסור להחנות לצד מתקן האש למקרי שריפה.
When there is a fire, the first to arrive on scene are the firemen.
Bezman sreifa harishonim lahag'ee'ya la makom em ha kabahiim.
בזמן שריפה הראשונים להגיע למקום הם הכבאים.
In an emergency situation everyone needs to be rescued.
Be mikrei cheiroom koolam zkook'eem le hatzala.
במקרי חירום כולם זקוקים להצלה.
The gas explosion led to a natural disaster.
Pi-tzootz ha gaz garam (led to) le ason teva.
פציוץ הגאז גרם לאסון טבע
During a siren you need to run to the bomb shelter.
Bezman ha aza'aka (alarm) ata tzarich larutz la miklat.
בזמן האזעקה אתה צריך לרוץ למקלט
This is a disaster area, therefore there is a mandatory evacuation order.
Ze ezor ha ason, lachen yesh tzav (an order) pinui chova.
זה אזור האסון, לכן יש צו פינוי חובה.

Overflow (water) – Hatzafa - הצפה
Storm - Soofa סופה
Storm - Se'aara – סערה
Snowstorm - Sufat shlag'iim – סופת שלגים
Hail – Barad - ברד
Bomb shelter – Miklat – מקלט
Refuge – Chasoot - חסות
Cause – Grima - גרימה
Safety – Betichoot - בטיחות
Drought - Batzoret - בצורת
Famine - Ra'av - רעב
Poverty - Onn'ee - עוני
Epidemic - Mag'efa - מגיפה
Pandemic - Pandemee'ya – פנדמייה
Earthquake - Reidat hadama – רעידת אדמה

The hurricane caused a lot of damage and destruction in its path.
Ha hurican garam le nezek ve le eres gadol (massive) bae darko (its path).
ההוריקן גרם לנזק ולהרס גדול בדרכו.
The tornado destroyed the town.
Ha tornado haras et ha ay'ara.
הטורנדו הרס את העיירה
The drought led to famine and a lot of poverty.
Ha batzoret oviila le raav ve harbei onn'ee.
הבצורת הובילה לרעב והרבה עוני.
There were three days of flooding following the storm.
Hayu shlosha yamei sheetafon behikvot (following) ha se'ara.
היו שלושה ימי שיטפון בעקבות הסערה.
This is a snowstorm and not a hail storm.
Zo sufat sheleg ve lo sufat barad.
זו סופת שלג ולא סופת ברד.
We need to stay in a safe place during the earthquake.
Aleinu lehishaher bae makom batuach bezman reidat ha hadama
עלינו להישאר במקום בטוח בזמן רעידת האדמה.

Blackout - Afsakat chashmal – הפסקת חשמל
Rainstorm - Mabul – מבול
Rainstorm - Sufat gshamiim – סופת גשמים
Avalanche - Mapolet shlag'iim – מפולת שלגים
Heatwave - Gal chom – גל חום
Rip current – Zerem - זרם
Tsunami – Tzunamee - צונאמי
Whirlpool - Ma'arbolet - מערבולת
Lightning - Barak - ברק
Lightning - (plural) brak'iim – ברקים
Thunder - Ra'am - רעם
Danger - Sakana - סכנה
Dangerous – Mesookan - מסוכן
A warning - Hazhara - אזהרה
Warning! - Zehirut! - זהירות

There was a blackout for three hours due to the rainstorm.
Shalosh shahot a'ita hafsakat chashmal biglal sufat hagshamiim.
שלוש שעות הייתה הפסקת חשמל בגלל סופת הגשמים.
Be careful during the snowstorm, because there might be an avalanche. Hizaher/hizaheri bezman sufat ha shlag'iim ki alula laredet mapolet shlag'iim.
היזהר\היזהרי בזמן סופת הגשמים כי עלולה לרדת מפולת שלגים.
There is a tsunami warning today.
Hayom yesh hazhara le tzunami.
היום יש אזהרה לצונאמי.
You can't swim against a rip current.
Eincha/einech yachol/yechola lischot neged ha zerem.
אֵינְךָ\אֵינֵךְ יכול\יכולה לשחות נגד הזרם.
There is a dangerous whirlpool in the ocean.
Yesh ma'arbolet mesukenet ba yam.
יש מערבולת מסוכנת בים.
There is a risk of lightning today.
Yesh sikun le soofat brak'iim hayom.
יש סיכון לסופת ברקים.
Heatwaves are usually in the summer.
Galei chom hem bederech klal ba kaitz.
גלי חום הם בדרך כלל בקיץ.

HOME - BA'IIT - בית

Living room - Chadar orchim – חדר אורחים
Couch – Sapa - ספה
Sofa – Koorsa - כורסה
Door - De'let - דלת
Closet - A'ron - ארון
Stairway – Madregot - מדרגות
Rug – Shatiach - שטיח
Curtain - Vee'lon - וילון
Window – Chalon - חלון
Floor – Ritzpa - רצפה
Floor (as in level) - Ko'ma - קומה
Candle – Ner - נר

The living room is missing a couch and a sofa.
Ba salon chaseriim (missing) sapa ve koorsa.
בסלון חסרים ספה וכורסה.
I must buy a new door for my closet.
Alai liknot de'let chadasha la a'ron
עליי לקנות דלת חדשה לארון.
The spiral staircase is beautiful.
Ha madregot ha loli'ya'nyot yafot me'od.
המדרגות הלולייניות יפות מאוד.
There aren't any curtains on the windows.
Ein veelonot la chalonot.
אין וילונות לחלונות.
I have a marble floor on the first floor and a wooden floor on the second floor.
Yesh li ritzpat shaiish bakoma harishona ve ritzpat etz ba koma ha shnee'ya.
יש לי רצפת שייש בקומה הראשונה ורצפת עץ בקומה השנייה.
I can only light this candle now.
Ani yachol/yechola lahadlik et ha ner hazei achshav.
אני יכול\יכולה להדליק את הנר הזה עכשיו.
I can clean the floors today and then I want to arrange the closet.
Ani yachol lenakot et haritzpa hayom ve az ani rotzei lesader et ha a'ron.
אני יכול לנקות את הרצפה היום ואז אני רוצה לסדר את הארון.

Silverware - Sak'oom – סכו"ם
Knife – Sakiin - סכין
Spoon - Kaaf - כף
Fork – Mazleg - מזלג
Teaspoon – Kapit - כפית
Kitchen – Mitbach - מטבח
A cup/mug – Seffel - ספל
Plate – Tzalachat - צלחת
Bowl - Ke'ara - קערה
Little bowl - Ke'arit - קערית
Napkin - Maap'eet - מפית
Table – Shulchan - שולחן
Placemat - Sha'ha'vaneet - מצעית
Fireplace – Ach - אח / **Chimney** – Arooba - ארובה
Laundry detergent - Sabon kviisa – סבון כביסה

The knives, spoons, teaspoons, and forks are inside the drawer in the kitchen.
Ha sakiniim, ha mazlegot, ha kap'ot, ve ha kapiyot nimtzahiim (situated) betoch ha meg'eera ba mitbach.
הסכינים, המזלגות, הכפות והכפיות נמצאים בתוך המגירה במטבח.

There aren't enough cups, plates, and silverware on the table for everyone.
Ein maspik kossot, tzalachot, ve sak'oom al ha shulchan le koolam.
אין מספיק כוסות, צלחות וסכו"ם על השולחן לכולם.

The napkin is underneath the bowl.
Ha maapeet mitachat la kei'ara.
המפית מתחת לקערה.

The placemats are on the table.
Ha shavanee'yot hen al ha shoolchan.
המטליות הן על השולחן.

The fire sparkles in the fireplace.
Ha esh (fire) notzetzet (sparkles) ba ach.
האש נוצצת באח.

I have to wash the rug with laundry detergent.
Ani tzarich/tzreicha lirchotz et ha shatiiach iim sabon kvisa.
אני צריך\צריכה לרחוץ את השטיח עם סבון כביסה.

Table cloth - Mapat ha Shulchan – מפת השולחן
Glass (material) – Zchoochit – זכוכית
A glass (cup) – Koss - כוס
Oven – Tanoor - תנור
Stove – Keera - כירה
Pot (cooking) – Seer - סיר
Pan – Machvat - מחבת
Shelve – Madaf - מדף
Cabinet - A'ron mitbach – ארון מטבח
Pantry - Mae'za'vei - מזוה
Drawer - Meg'eera - מגירה

The table cloth is beautiful.
Mapat ha shoolchan yafa.
מפת השולחן יפה.
There is canned food in the pantry.
Ba mae'zavei yesh shimurrim (canned food).
במזוה יש שימורים.
Where are the toothpicks?
Eifo ha kis'miim?
איפה הקיסמים?
The glasses on the shelve are used for champagne, not wine.
Ha kosot ba madaf hen le shampanya, lo leyaiin.
הכוסות במדף הן לשמפניה, לא ליין.
The pizza is in the oven.
Ha pizza ba tanoor.
הפיצה בתנור.
The pots and pans are in the cabinet.
Ha seer'eem ve ha machvatot ba a'ron.
הסירים והמחבתות בארון.
The stove isn't functioning.
Ha keera lo po'elet.
הקערה לא פועלת.

Bedroom - Chadar sheina – חדר שינה
Bed – Meeta - מיטה
Mattress – Mizron - מזרון
Blanket – Smicha - שמיכה
Bed sheet – Sadiin - סדין
Pillow – Kariit - כרית
Mirror - Mar'a – מראה
Chair - Ki'sei – כיסא
Dining room - Chadar ochel – חדר אוכל
Hallway - Misdaron – מסדרון
Hallway - Prozdor – פרוזדור
Downstairs – Lemata - למטה
Trash - Zevel – זבל
Trash - Ashpa – אשפה
Garbage can - Pach ashpa – פח אשפה
Garbage can - pach zevel – פח זבל

The master bedroom is at the end of the hallway, and the dining room is downstairs.
Chadar ha sheina nimtza besof ha prozdor, ve chadar ha ochel nimtza lemata.
חדר השינה נמצא בסוף הפרוזדור וחדר האוכל נמצא למטה.
The mirror looks good in the bedroom.
Ha mar'aa nir'et (looks/seems) tov ba chadar ha sheina.
המראה נראית טוב בחדר השינה
I have to buy a new bed and a new mattress.
Ani tzarich/tzreicha liknot meeta ve mizron chadashiim.
אני צריך\צריכה לקנות מיטה ומזרון חדשים.
Where are the blankets and bed sheets?
Eifo ha smichot ve ha sdiniim?
איפה השמיכות והסדינים?
My pillows are on the chair.
Ha kariyot sheli al ha kisei.
הכריות שלי על הכיסא.
The garbage can is blocking the driveway.
Pach ha ashpa chosem (blocking) et shvil ha kneesa.
פח האשפה חוסם את שביל הכניסה.

Towel - Mag'evet – מגבת
Bathroom - Chadar sherutiim – חדר שירותים
Bathtub - Ambat'ya - אמבטיה
Shower – Miklachat - מקלחת
Sink - Ki'yor - כיור
Faucet – Berez - ברז
Soap – Sabon - סבון
Bag – Sakiit - שקית
Box - Kufsa - קופסא
Box - Argaz - ארגז
Key - Mafteia'ch - מפתח

These towels are for drying your hand.
Ha magavot ha elu hen leyebush yadaiim.
המגבות האלו הן לייבוש ידיים.
The bathtub, shower, and the sink are old.
Ha ambatya, ha miklachat, ve ha ki'yor yeshaniim.
האמבטיה, המקלחת והכיור ישנים.
I need soap to wash my hands.
Ani tzarich sabon kedi lirchotz et ha yadiim.
אני צריך סבון כדי לרחוץ את הידיים.
The guest bathroom is in the corner of the hallway.
Ha shiruttim shel ha orchiim nimtzahiim bae pinat (corner) ha misdaron.
השירותים של האורחים נמצאים בפינת המסדרון.
How many boxes does he have?
Kama kufsa'ott yesh lo?
כמה קופסאות יש לו?
I want to put my things in the plastic bag.
Ani rotzei/rotza lassiim et ha dvariim sheli bae sakiit plastic.
אני רוֹצֶה\רוֹצָה לשים את הדברים שלי בשקית פלסטיק.
I need to bring my keys.
Ani tzarich/tzreicha lahavi et ha mafte'chot sheli.
אני צריך\צריכה להביא את המפתחות שלי.

Room – Cheder - חדר
Balcony – Mirpeset - מרפסת
Roof - Ga'g - גג
Ceiling – Tikra – תקרה
Wall – Keer - קיר
Carpet – Shatiach – שטיח
Attic - Aliyat ga'g – עליית גג
Basement – Martef – מרתף
Driveway - Shvil ha kneesa – שביל הכניסה
Garden – Guina - גינה
Backyard – Chatzer - חצר
Jar - Tzin'tzenet - צנצנת
Doormat – Machtzelet - מחצלת

I can install new windows for my balcony.
Ani yachol lahatkiin chalonot chadashim la mirpeset sheli.
אני יכול להתקין חלונות חדשים למפרסת שלי.

I must install a new roof.
Ani chayav le'atkiin ga'g chadash.
אני חייב להתקין גג חדש.

The color of my ceiling is white.
Tzeva ha tikra sheli lavan.
צבע התקרה שלי לבן.

I must paint the walls.
Ani chayav litzboha et ha kirot.
אני חייב לצבוע את הקירות

The attic is an extra room in the house.
Aliyat ha ga'g hee cheder nosaf babaiit.
עליית הגג היא חדר נוסף בבית.

The kids are playing either in the basement or the backyard.
Hayeladiim mesa'chakeem ba martef o ba chatzer.
הילדים משחקים במרתף או בחצר.

All the glass jars are outside on the doormat.
Kol ha tzin'tzanot nimtzahot bachutz al ha machtzelet.
כל הצנצנות נמצאות בחוץ על המחצלת.

Conclusion

You have now learned a wide range of sentences in relation to a variety of topics such as the home and garden. You can discuss the roof and ceiling of a house, plus natural disasters like hurricanes and thunderstorms.

The combination of sentences can also work well when caught in a natural disaster and having to deal with emergency issues. When the electricity gets cut you can tell your family or friends, "I can only light this candle now." As you're running out of the house, remind yourself of the essentials by saying, "I need to bring my keys with me."

If you need to go to a hospital, you have now been provided with sentences and the vocabulary for talking to doctors and nurses and dealing with surgery and health issues. Most importantly, you can ask, "What is the emergency number in this country?" When you get to the hospital, tell the health services, "The hurricane caused a lot of destruction and damage in its path," and "We used the hurricane shelter for refuge."

The three hundred and fifty words that you learned in part 1 should have been a big help to you with these new themes. When learning the Hebrew language, you are now more able to engage with people in Hebrew, which should make your travels flow a lot easier.

Part 3 will introduce you to additional topics that will be invaluable to your journeys. You will learn vocabulary in relation to politics, the military, and the family. The three books in this series all together provide a flawless system of learning the Hebrew language. When you visit Israel, you will now have the capacity for greater conversational learning.

When you proceed to Part 3 you will be able to expand your vocabulary and conversational skills even further. Your range of topics will expand to the office environment, business negotiations and even school.

Please, feel free to post a review in order to share your experience or suggest feedback as to how this method can be improved.

Conversational Hebrew Quick and Easy
The Most Innovative Technique to Learn the Hebrew Language

Part III

YATIR NITZANY

Translated by:
Semadar Mercedes Friedman

Introduction to the Program

You have now reached Part 3 of Conversational Hebrew Quick and Easy. In Part 1 you learned the 350 words that could be used in an infinite number of combinations. In Part 2 you moved on to putting these words into sentences. You learned how to ask for help when your house was hit by a hurricane and how to find the emergency services. For example, if you need to go to a hospital, you have now been provided with sentences and the vocabulary for talking to doctors and nurses and dealing with surgery and health issues. When you get to the hospital, you can tell the health services, "The hurricane caused a lot of destruction and damage in its path," and "We used the hurricane shelter for refuge."

In this third book in the series, you will find the culmination of this foreign language course that is based on a system using key phrases used in day-to-day life. You can now move on to further topics such as things you would say in an office. This theme is ideal if you've just moved to Hebrew for a new job. You may be about to sit at your desk to do an important task assigned to you by your boss but you have forgotten the details you were given. Turn to your colleagues and say, "I have to write an important email but I forgot my password." Then, if the reply is "Our secretary isn't here today. Only the receptionist is here but she is in the bathroom," you'll know what is being said and you can wait for help. By the end of the first few weeks, you'll have at your disposal terminology that can help reflect your experiences. "I want to retire already," you may find yourself saying at coffee break on a Monday morning after having had to go to your bank manager and say, "I need a small loan in order to pay my mortgage this month."

I came up with the idea of this unique system of learning foreign languages as I was struggling with my own attempt to learn Hebrew. When playing around with word combinations I discovered 350 words that when used together could make up an infinite number of sentences. From this beginning, I was able to start speaking in a new language. I then practiced and found that I could use the same technique with other languages, such as French, Hebrew, Italian and Arabic. It was a revelation.

This method is by far the easiest and quickest way to master other languages and begin practicing conversational language skills.

The range of topics and the core vocabulary are the main components of this flawless learning method. In Part 3 you have a chance to learn how to relate to people in many more ways. Sports, for example, are very important for keeping healthy and in good spirits. The social component of these types of activities should not be underestimated at all. You will, therefore, have much help when you meet some new people, perhaps in a bar, and want to say to them, "I like to watch basketball games," and "Today are the finals of the Olympic Games. Let's see who wins the World Cup."

For sports, the office, and for school, some parts of conversation are essential. What happens when you need to get to work but don't have any clean clothes to wear because of malfunctions with the machinery. What you need is to be able to pick up the phone and ask a professional or a friend, "My washing machine and dryer are broken so maybe I can wash my laundry at the public laundromat." When you finally head out after work for some drinks and meet a nice new man, you can say, "You can leave me a voicemail or send me a text message."

Hopefully, these examples help show you how reading all three parts of this series in combination will prepare you for all you need in order to boost your conversational learning skills and engage with others in your newly learned language. The first two books have been an important start. This third book adds additional vocabulary and will provide the comprehensive knowledge required.

OFFICE – MISRAD - משרד

Office – Misrad - משרד
Boss - (male/zachar) Ba'al ha esek – בעל העסק
Boss – (female/nekeva) ba'alat ha esek – בעלת העסק
Employee - Sachiir - שכיר
Employee – (female) schiira - שכירה
Staff – Tzevet - צוות
Meeting - Mifgash מפגש
Meeting - Pgisha – פגישה
Conference room - Chadar yeshivot – חדר ישיבות
Secretary - Maskira - מזכירה
Receptionist - Pkidat kabala – פקידת קבלה
Schedule - Luach ha zmaniim לוח הזמנים
Schedule - Maharechet ha zmaniim – מערכת הזמנים
Calendar - Luach ha shana – לוח השנה

My boss asked me to hand in the paperwork.
Ha menahel bikesh mimeni lehageesh lo et ha nayeret.
המנהל ביקש ממני להגיש לו את הניירת.

Our secretary isn't here today. The receptionist is here but she is in the bathroom.
Ha mazkira shelano lo kan hayom. Pkidat-ha kabala kan aval hee ba sherootim.
המזכירה שלנו לא כאן היום. פקידת הקבלה כאן אבל היא בשירותים.

The employee meeting can take place in the conference room.
Pg'ishat ha ovdiim yechola lehitkayem (to take place) ba chadar ha yeshiv'ott.
פגישת העובדים יכולה להתקיים בחדר הישיבות.

My business cards are inside my briefcase.
Kartisei ha bikoor sheli hem bae yalkoot ha mismacheem sheli.
כרטיסי הביקור שלי הם בילקוט המסמכים שלי.

The office staff must check their work schedule daily.
Tzevet ha misrad chayav livdok et maharechet ha zmaniim shel ha avoda midei (each) yom.
צוות המשרד חייב לבדוק את מערכת הזמנים של העבודה מידי יום.

Supplies – Tziyood - ציוד
Pen – Ett - עט
Ink - Di'yo - דיו
Pencil – Eeparon - עיפרון
Eraser – Mochek - מחק
Desk - Machteva - מכתבה
Cubicle – Ta - תא
Chair - Kees'ei - כיסא
Office furniture - Ri'hoot misradee – ריהוט משרדי
Business card - Kartiis bikoor – כרטיס ביקור
Lunch break - Afsakat tzo'hora'eem – הפסקת צהריים
Days off - Yamei choofsha – ימי חופשה
Briefcase - Yalkoot mismacheem – ילקוט מסמכים
Bathroom – Sherootim - שירותים

I am going to buy office furniture.
Ani **(male)**olech/**(female)**olechet liknot ri'hoot misradee.
אני הולך\הולכת לקנות ריהוט משרדי.

There isn't any ink in this pen.
Eiin di'yo ba ett hazei.
אין דיו בעט הזה.

This pencil is missing an eraser.
La eeparon hazei chaser (missing) mochek.
לעיפרון הזה חסר מוחק.

Our days off are written on the calendar.
Yamei ha choofsha shelanu ktoovim (are written) al luach ha shana.
ימי החופשה שלנו כתובים על לוח השנה.

I need to buy extra office supplies.
Ani **(male)**tzarich/**(female)**tzreicha liknot tziyood misradee nosaf (extra).
אני צריך\צריכה לקנות ציוד משרדי נוסף.

I am busy until my lunch break.
Ani asook/asooka aad afsakat ha tzo'hora'iim.
אני עסוק\עסוקה עד הפסקת הצהריים.

Laptop - Mach'shev nayad – מחשב נייד
Computer - Mach'shev - מחשב
Keyboard – Makledet - מקלדת
Mouse – Achbar - עכבר
Email - Email אימייל
Email - Doo'el (do'ar electron'ee) – (דואר אלקטרוני) דוא"ל
Password – Sisma - סיסמא
Attachment - Kovetz-metzoraf – קובץ מצורף
Printer – Matpeset - מדפסת
Colored printer - Matpeset tziv'oniit – מדפסת צבעונית

I want to write an important email but I forgot my password for my account.
Ani **(m)**rotzei/**(f)**rotza lichtov email chashoov (important) aval shachachtee et ha sisma shel ha cheshbon sheli.
אני רוֹצָה\רוֹצָה לכתוב אימייל חשוב אבל שכחתי את הסיסמא של החשבון שלי.

I need to purchase a computer, a keyboard, a printer, and a desk.
Ani tzarich/tzreicha liknot machshev, makledet, matpeset, ve machteva.
אני צריך\צריכה לקנות מחשב, מקלדת, מדפסת ומכתבה.

Where is the mouse on my laptop?
Eifo ha achbar shel ha machshev ha nayad sheli?
איפה העכבר של המחשב הנייד שלי.

Do you have a colored printer?
Yesh (m)lecha/(f)lach matpeset tziv'oneet?
יש לְךָ\לָךְ מדפסת צבעונית?

I needed to fax the contract but instead, I decided to send it as an attachment in the email.
Ani hayiti tzarich/tzreicha lefakses et ha chozei aval bimkom hechlateti lishloach oto ke-kovetz-metzoraf la email.
אני הייתי צריך\צריכה לפקסס את החוזה אבל במקום החלטתי לשלוח.

To download – Lehorid - להוריד
To upload - Le'ha'a lot - לעלות
Internet – Internet - אינטרנט
Account – Cheshbon - חשבון
A copy - Ha'etek - העתק
To copy - Leha'ateek - להעתיק
Paste – Lehadbeek - להדביק
Fax – Fax - פקס
Scanner – Sorek - סורק
To scan – Lisrok - לסרוק
Telephone – Teléfon - טלפון
Charger - Matt'en - מטען
To charge (a phone) - Lehat'een - להטעין

The internet is slow today therefore it's difficult to upload or download.
Ha internet eetii (slow) hayom ve-lachen (and therefore) kashei le'ha'alot hoo lehoreed.
האינטרנט איטי היום ולכן קשה לעלות או להוריד.

One day, the fax machine will be completely obsolete.
Yom echad mechonat ha faks teehe'yae mae-yoo-tarot (obsolete) lechalooteen (completely).
יום אחד יום אחד מכונת הפאקס תהיה מיותרת לחלוטין.

Where is my phone charger?
Eifo mat'hen ha telefon sheli?
איפה מטען הטלפון שלי?

The scanner is broken.
Ha sorek shavoor (broken).
הסורק שבור.

The telephone is behind the chair.
Ha telefon nimtza me'achorei (behind) ha kisei.
הטלפון נמצא מאחורי הכיסא.

Shredder – Magrasa - מגרסה
Copy machine - Mechonat tzi'loom מכונת צילום
Copy machine - Mechonat ha'atakah – מכונת העתקה
Filing cabinet - A'ron tiyook – ארון תיוק
Paper - Neyar נייר
Papers - Neyarot – ניירות
Page - Daaf דף
Pages - Dappiim – דפים
Paperwork – Nayeret - ניירת
Portfolio – Oogdan - אוגדן
Files – Kvatzim - קבצים
Document – Mismach - מסמך
Deadline - Mo'ed acharon – מועד אחרון

The copy machine is next to the telephone.
Mechonat ha tziloom leyad (next to) ha telefon.
.מכונת הצילום ליד הטלפון

I can't find my stapler, paper clips, nor my highlighter in my cubicle.
Ani lo yachol limtzo et ha mehadek, et ha sikot, ve lo et ett ha sim'oon sheli ba ta sheli.
.אני לא יכול למצוא את המהדק, את הסיכות ולא את עט הסימון שלי בתא שלי

The filing cabinet is full of documents.
A'ron ha tiyook malei-bei (full of) mismachiim.
.ארון התיוק מלא במסמכים

The garbage can is full.
Paach ha ashpa malei.
.פח האשפה מלא

Give me the file because today is the deadline.
Ten-lee (give me) et ha teek ki hayom hoo ha mohed ha acharon.
.תן לי את התיק כי היום הוא המועד האחרון

Contract – Chozae - חוזה
Records – Reshimot - רשימות
Archives – Archyoon - ארכיון
Binder – Ogdan - אוגדן
Paper clip - Atav nee'yar – אטב נייר
Stapler – Mahadek sikot - מהדק סיכות
Staples – Mehadkeem - מהדקים
Stamp – Bool - בול
Mail - Do'ar - דואר
Letter – Michtav - מכתב
Envelope - Ma'atafa - מעטפה
Data - Da'ta - דאתא
Data - Maydaa – מידע
Analysis - Neetoo'ach - ניתוח
Highlighter - Ett sim'oon – עט סימון
To highlight – Lesamen - לסמן
Marker – Mesamen - מסמן
Ruler - Sarg'el - סרגל

The supervisor at our company is responsible for data analysis.
Mefakei'ach ha chevra shelanoo achra'ee al neetoo'ach ha maydaa.
מפקח החברה שלנו אחראי על ניתוח המידע.

Where do I put the binder?
Eefo laseem et ha oogdan?
איפה לשים את האוגדן?

The ruler is next to the shredder.
Ha sarg'el nimtza leyad ha magresa.
הסרגל נמצא ליד המגרסה.

I need a stamp and an envelope.
Ani tzarich/treicha bool hoo mahatafa.
אני צריך\צריכה בול ומעטפה.

There is a letter in the mail.
Yesh michtav ba do'ar.
יש מכתב בדואר.

SCHOOL - BEIT SEFER – בית ספר

Student – Talmid - תלמיד
Student – (f) Talmida - תלמידה
Students – (p) Talmidiim - תלמידים
Teacher – Morei - מוֹרֶה
Teacher – (f) Mora - מוֹרָה
Substitute teacher - Memalei makom – ממלאי מקום
A class – Shihoor - שיעור
A classroom – Keeta - כיתה
Education – Chinooch - חינוך

The classroom is empty.
Ha kita reika (empty).
הכיתה ריקה.

I want to bring my laptop to class.
Ani rotzei lahavi eeti (with me) et machshev ha nayad sheli la kita.
אני רוצה להביא איתי את מחשב הנייד שלי לכיתה.

Our math teacher is absent and therefore a substitute teacher replaced him.
Ha morei shelano le matematica lo kan hayom ve lachen mora ha machlifa hechlifa oto.
המורה שלנו למתמטיקה לא כאן היום ולכן המחליפה החליפה אותו.

All the students are present.
Kol ha talmidiim nochaciim.
כל התלמידים נוכחים.

Make sure to pass your classes because you can't fail this semester.
Tid'ag (make sure) lahavor et kol ha kitoot shelcha mikevan shae ata lo yachol leikashel ba samester hazei.
תדאג לעבור את כל הכיתות שלך מכיוון שאתה לא יכול להיכשל בסמסטר הזה.

The education level at a private school is much more intense.
Ramat ha chinooch bae beit sefer prati arbei yoter intensivit.
רמת החינוך בבית ספר פרטי הרבה יותר אינטנסיבית.

Private school - Beit sefer prati – בית ספר פרטי
Public school - Beit sefer tziboori – בית ספר ציבורי
Elementary school - Beit sefer yesodee – בית ספר יסודי
Middle school - Chativat beiy'nay'eem – חטיבת ביניים
High school - Beit sefer tichon – בית ספר תיכון
University – Ooniversita - אוניברסיטה
College – Michlala - מכללה
Grade (level) – Kita - כיתה
Grade (grade on a test) - Tzi'yoon - ציון
Pass – Avar - עבר
Fail – Nichshal - נכשל
Absent – Chaser - חסר
Present – Nochach - נוכח

I went to a public elementary and middle school.
Lamadeti bae beit sefer yesodi tzibori ve bae chativat beiy'nay'eem tzibori.
למדתי בבית ספר יסודי ציבורי ובחטיבת ביניים ציבורי.

I have good memories of high school.
Yesh li zichronot (memories) tovot mei beit ha sefer tichon.
יש לי זכרונות טובים מבית הספר התיכון.

My son is 15 years old and he is in the ninth grade.
Ha ben sheli ben-chameshesrei (15 years old) ve hoo bae kita tet (ninth).
הבן שלי בן חמש עשרה והוא בכיתה ט'.

You must get good grades on your report card.
Aleicha lekabel tziyoniim toviim ba tehuda shelcha.
עליך לקבל ציונים טובים בתעודה שלך.

College textbooks are expensive.
Sifrei limood ba michlala em yekariim (expensive).
סיפרי לימוד במכללה הם יקרים.

I want to study at an out-of-state university.
Ani rotzei/rotza lilmod bae universita mechootz-la (outside of) medina.
אני רוֹצָה\רוֹצָה ללמוד באוניברסיטה מחוץ למדינה.

Subject - Nos'ae - נושא
Lesson - Shi'oor - שיעור
Science – Mada - מדע
Chemistry - Cheem'ee'ya - כימיה
Physics – Physica - פיזיקה
Geography - Guio'grafi'ya - גיאוגרפיה
History - Histor'ya - היסטוריה
Math - Cheshbon חשבון
Mathematics - Matemática מתממטיקה
Addition – Chiboor - חיבור
Subtraction – Chisoor - חיסור
Division – Chilook - חילוק
Multiplication – Kefel - כפל

At school, geography is my favorite class, English is easy, math is hard, and history is boring.
Bae beit ha sefer guio'grafi'ya ha shihoor ha hahoov (favorite) alai, anglit kal, matematika kashei, ve historya meshahamem (boring).
בבית הספר גיאוגרפיה השיעור האהוב עליי, אנגלית קל, מתממטיקה קשה והיסטוריה משעמם.

After English class, there is physical education.
Achrei shihoor anglit yesh itamloot.
אחרי שיעור אנגלית יש התעמלות.

Today's math lesson is on addition and subtraction. Next month it will be division and multiplication.
Shihoor ha matematika hayom mevusas-al (based on) chiboor ve chisoor. Ba chodesh (month) haba (next) chilook ve kifool.
שיעור המתממטיקה היום מבוסס על חיבור וחיסור. בחודש הבא חילוק וכיפול.

The teacher wants to teach the students roman numerals.
Ha mora rotza leilamed et ha talmidiim ba sfarot romiyot.
המורה רוצה ללמד את התלמידים בספרות רומיות.

Language – Safa - שפה
English – Anglit - אנגלית
Foreign language - Safa zara – שפה זרה
Physical education - Shi'oor eetamloot – שיעור התעמלות
Chalk - G'iir - גיר
Board – Luach - לוח
Report card – Tehuda - תעודה
Alphabet - Alef-bet – אלף-בית
Letters - Oti'yot - אותיות
Words - Mi'leem - מילים
Vocabulary - Otzar milim - אוצר מילים
To review - Lachzor al – לחזור על
Dictionary – Milon - מילון
Detention – Reetook - ריתוק
The principle – Menahel - מנהל
The principle – (f) Menahelet - מנהלת

This year for foreign language credits, I want to choose Spanish and French.
Ha shana havoor (towards) nekudat-zchoot (credit) ba safa zara, ani rotzei lilmod sfaradiit ve tzarfateet.
השנה עבור נקודת זכות בשפה זרה, אני רוצה ללמוד ספרדית וצרפתית.
I want to buy a dictionary, thesaurus, and a journal for school.
Ani rotzei/rotza liknot milon, tzoroos, ve yoman la limoodiim.
אני רוֹצֶה\רוֹצָה לקנות מילון, תזאורוס ויומן ללימודים.
The teacher needs to write the homework on the board with chalk.
Ha morei tzarich lichtov et ha shihoorei bait bei giir al ha luach.
המורה צריך לכתוב את השיעורי בית בגיר על הלוח.
Today the students have to review the letters of the alphabet.
Hayom ha talmidiim chayaviim lachzor al otiyoot ha alef bet.
היום תלמידים חייבים לחזור על אותיות האלף-בית.
If you can't behave well then you must go to the principal's office, and maybe stay after school for detention.
Eem ata lo yachol leihtnaheg yafei az alecha lageshet la misrad ha menahel ve olai leeishaher achrei beit sefer..
אם אתה לא יכול להתנהג יפה אז עליך לגשת למשרד המנהל ואולי להישאר אחרי בית הספר.

Test – Mivchan - מבחן
Quiz - Bochan בוחן
Quiz - Chidon חידון
Notes – Reshimot - רשימות
Homework – Shi'hoo'reem - שיעורים
Assignment – Matala- מטלה
Project – Proyect - פרויקט
Backpack - Tarmil תרמיל / **Backpack -** Teek gav תיק גב
Notebook – Machberet - מחברת
Crayons – Efronot tzivoneem - עפרונות ציבעוניים
Lunchbox - Koofsat ochel – קופסאת אוכל
Glue – Devek - דבק
Scissors – Misparaiim - מספריים

Today, we don't have a test but we have a surprise quiz.
Hayom ein-lanu (we don't have) mivchan aval yesh lanu bochan afta'ha.
.היום אין לנו מבחן אבל יש לנו בוחן הפתעה

Are a pen, a pencil, and an eraser included with the school supplies?
Haiim et, iparon, ve mochek klooliim ba aspakat (supplies) beit ha sefer?
?האם עט, עיפרון ומוחק כלולים באספקת בית הספר

I think my notebook and calculator are in my backpack.
Ani choshev shae ha machberet ve ha machshevon nimtzaiim ba tarmil sheli.
.אני חושב שהמחברת והמחשבון נמצאים בתרמיל שלי

I need glue and scissors for my project.
Ani tzarich devek ve mispariim la proyect sheli.
.אני צריך דבק ומספריים לפרויקט שלי

I need tape and a stapler to fix my book.
Ani tzarich tzelotape ve mehadek kedei letaken et ha sefer sheli.
.אני צריך סלוטייפ ומהדק כדי לתקן את הספר שלי

You have to concentrate in order to take notes.
Ata tzarich leitrakez kedei lirshom reshimot.
.אתה צריך להתרכז כדי לרשום רשימות

I forgot my lunchbox and crayons at home.
Shachachti et koofsat ha tzehoraiim ve et ha efronot sheli ba bait.
.שכחתי את קופסאת הצהריים ואת העפרונות שלי בבית

Folder - Teek'ee'ya - תיקייה
Papers - Dap'eem - דפים
Calculator – Machshevon - מחשבון
Adhesive tape – Tzelotape - סלוטייפ
Lunch - Aroochat tzhoraiim – ארוחת צהריים
Kindergarten - Gan chova – גן חובה
Pre-school - Trom chova – טרום חובה
Day care – Mahon yom – מעון יום
Triangle - Meshulash - משולש
Square - Ree'boo'aa - ריבוע
Circle – Eegool - עיגול

All my papers are in my folder.
Kol ha dapiim hem ba machberet sheli.
כל הדפים הם במחברת שלי.

The school librarian wants to invite the art and music teacher to the library next week.
Safranit (librarian) beit ha sefer rotza lehazmin et ha mora le omanut ve et mora le musica la sifriya (library) ba shavoa'a haba.
ספרנית בית הספר רוצה להזמין את המורה לאומנות ואת המורה למוזיקה לספריה בשבוע הבא.

For lunch, your children can purchase food at the cafeteria or they can bring food from home.
Le aroochat ha tzhoraiim ha yeladim shelachem yecholim liknot ochel ba cafeteria o lahavi ochel mei ha bait.
לארוחת הצהריים הילדים שלכם יכולים לקנות אוכל בקפיטריה או להביא אוכל מהבית.

To draw shapes such as a triangle, square, circle, and rectangle is easy.
Kal (easy) letzayer tzoorot kmo (such) meshulash, reebo'ha, eegool, ve malben.
קל לצייר צורות כמו משולש, ריבוע, עיגול ומלבן.

During the week, my youngest child is at daycare, my middle one is in pre-school, and the oldest is in kindergarten.
Bae-mahalach (throughout) ha shavoa'a ha yeled ha tzaiir sheli nimtza ba ma'aon yom, beni ha emtzaii ba gan, ve ha ben habechor nimtza ba gan chova.
במהלך השבוע הילד הצעיר שלי נמצא במעון יום, בני האמצעי בגן והבן הבכור נמצא בגן חובה.

PROFESSION - MIKTZOA'A - מקצוע

Psychologist – Psicholog - פסיכולוג
Psychologist – (f)Psicholog'eet - פסיכולוגית
Psychiatrist - Psichi'ater - פסיכיאטר
Veterinarian - Veterinar - וטרינר
Veterinarian - (f) Veterinareet - וטרינרית
Lawyer - Orech deen עורך דין / **Lawyer** - Prak'leetan פרקליטן
Judge – Shofet - שופט
Judge – (f) shofetet - שופטת
Pilot – Tayas - טייס
Pilot – (f) tayeset - טייסת
Flight attendant – Dayal – דייל
Flight attendant – (f) Dayelet - דיילת

What's your profession?
Ma ha miktzoa'a shelcha/shelach?
מה המקצוע שֶׁלְךָ\שֶׁלָךְ?
I'm going to med school to study medicine since I want to be a doctor.
Ani olech/olechet lebeit sefer lerefoha ki ani rotzei/rotza leiyot rofei/rofa.
אני הולך\הולכת לבית ספר לרפואה כי אני רוֹצֶה\רוֹצָה להיות רופא\רופאה.
There is a difference between a psychologist and a psychiatrist.
Yesh evdel (difference) ben pischolog ve psychiater.
יש הבדל בין פסיכולוג ופסיכיאטר.
Most children want to be astronauts, veterinarians, or athletes.
Rov ha yeladiim rotzim liyot astronaut'eem, veterinar'eem, o sporta'eem.
רוב הילדים רוצים להיות אסטרונאוטים, וטרינרים, או ספורטאים.
The judge spoke to the lawyer at the court house.
Ha shofet sochei'ach eem ha orech'deen ba beit-ha-mishpat (court house).
השופט שוחח עם העורך דין בבית המשפט.
Are you a photographer?
Ha'iim ata/att tzalam/tzalemet?
האם אתה\את צלם\צלמת.
The flight attendant and the pilot are on the plane.
Ha dayal ve ha tayas nimtzaheem al ha matos.
הדייל והטייס נמצאים על המטוס.

Reporter – Katav - כתב
Reporter – (f) Katevet - כתבת
Journalist - Eetona'ee - עיתונאי
Journalist - (f) Eetona'eet - עיתונאית
Electrician - Chashmela'ee - חשמלאי
Mechanic - Mechona'ee - מכונאי
Investigator – Choker - חוקר
Investigator – (f) Chokeret - חוקרת
Detective – Balash - בלש
Translator - Metarg'em - מתרגם
Translator - (f) Metarg'emet - מתרגמת
Producer – Mafeek - מפיק
Producer – (f) Mafeeka - מפיקה
Director – Menahel - מנהל

The police investigator needs to investigate this case.
Choker ha mishtara tzarich lachkor et ha meekrei (case) ha ze.
חוקר המשטרה צריך לחקור את המקרה הזה.

Being a detective could be a fun job.
Liyot balash yachol liyot avoda mehana (fun).
להיות בלש יכול להיות עבודה מהנה.

I am a certified electrician.
Ani chashmela'ee moos'mach (certified).
אני חשמלאי מוסמך.

The mechanic overcharged me.
Ha mechona'ee lakach mem'en'ee schar (payment) me'al (over) ha mekoobal (usual).
המכונאי לקח ממני שכר מעל המקובל.

I want to be a journalist.
Ani rotzei/rotza liyot eetona'ee/eetona'eet.
אני רוֹצֶה\רוֹצָה להיות עיתונאי\עיתונאית.

The best translators work at my company.
Meetav (the best/finest) ha metargem'eem ovdiim ba chevra sheli.
מיטב המתרגמים עובדים בחברה שלי.

I want to find the directors of the company.
Ani rotzei/rotza limtzo et menahel ha chevra.
אני רוֹצֶה\רוֹצָה את מנהל החברה.

Artist (performer) - Oman - אומן
Artist (performer) - **(f)** Oomaniit - אומנית
Artist (draws paints picture) - Tzayar - צייר
Artist (draws paints picture) - **(f)** Tzayariit - ציירת
Author – Sofer - סופר
Author – **(f)** Soferet - סופרת
Painter - Tzabai - צבעי
Painter - **(f)** Tzabahit - צבעית
Dancer - Rakdan - רקדן
Dancer - **(f)** Rakdaniit - רקדנית
Writer - Katav - כתב
Writer - **(f)** Kataviit - כתבית
Photographer – Tzalam - צלם
Photographer – **(f)** Tzalemet - צלמת
A cook – Tabach - טבח
A cook – **(f)** Tabachiit - טבחית
A chef - Tabach rashi – טבח ראשי
Waiter – Meltzar - מלצר
Waitress – Meltzariit - מלצרית
Bartender – Barmen - ברמן
Bartender – **(f)** Barmeniit - ברמנית

The artist drew a sketch.
Ha oman tzi'yer skitza (sketch).
האומן צייר סקיצה.
I want to apply as a cook at the restaurant instead of as a waiter.
Ani rotzei lahagish me'omad'oot kee tabach ba misa'adah bimkom ke meltzar.
אני רוצה להגיש מעומדות כטבח במסעדה במקום כמלצר.
The gardener can only come on weekdays.
Ha ganan yachol lavo rak bae yamei-chol (weekdays).
הגנן יכול לבוא רק בימי חול.
I have to go to the barbershop now.
Ani tzarich/tzreicha lalechet la maspera achshav.
אני צריך\צריכה ללכת למספרה עכשיו.
Being a bartender isn't an easy job.
Liyot barmen/barmeniit zot lo avoda kala.
להיות ברמן\ברמנית זאת לא עבודה קלה.

Barber - Sapar - ספר
Barber - (f) Sapariit - ספרית
Barber shop – Maspera - מספרה
Stylist - Meha'tzev sae'ar - מעצב שיער
Stylist - (f) Meha'tzevet sae'ar - מעצבת שיער
Maid – Ozeret - עוזרת
Housekeeper - Ozeret ba'itt – עוזרת בית
Caretaker – Metapel - מטפל
Caretaker – Metapelet - מטפלת
Farmer – Chakla'ee - חקלאי
Farmer – Eekar - איכאר
Gardner – Ganan - גנן
Mailman – Davar - דוור
A guard - Shomer - שומר
A guard - (f) shomeret - שומרת
Security guard - Iish bitachon - איש ביטחון
A cashier - Kupa'ee - קופאי
A cashier - (f) Kupa'eet - קופאית

Why do we need another maid?
Lama anu tzreichim ozeret acheret?
למה אנו צריכים עוזרת אחרת?
I want to file a complaint against the mailman.
Ani rotze/rotzei lahagish tloona (complaint) neg'ed ha do'ar.
אני רוצֶה\רוצָה להגיש תלונה נגד הדואר.
I am a part-time artist.
Ani tzayar bemiisra (shift) chelkiit (part-time).
אני צייר במשרה חלקית.
She was a dancer at the play.
Hee hayta rakdaniit ba atzaga.
היא הייתה רקדנית בהצגה.
You need to contact the insurance company if you want to find another caretaker.
Ata tzariich litzor kesher iim chevrat ha bitoach eem ata rotzei limtzo metapelet chadasha.
אתה צריך ליצור קשר עם חברת הביטוח אם אתה רוצה למצוא מטפלת חדשה.
The farmer can sell us ripened tomatoes today.
Ha eekar yachol limkor lanu (to us) agvanyot bshelot (ripened).
האיכאר יכול למכור לנו עגבניות בשלות.

BUSINESS - ASAK'EEM - עסקים

Business - Asak'eem - עסקים
A business - Essek - עסק
A business - (p) asakiim - עסקים
Company – Chevra - חברה
Factory - Mifhal - מפעל
Factory - Beit charoshet – בית חרושת
A professional – Miktzohee - מקצועי
Position - Misra - משרה
Work, job – Avoda - עבודה
Employee - Oved - עובד
Employee - (f) Ovedet - עובדת
Owner - Bahal ha esek - בעל העסק
Owner - Ba'al ha chevra – בעל החברה
Manager – Menahel - מנהל
Manager – (f) Menahelet - מנהלת
Management - An'hala - הנהלה
Secretary – Maskira - מזכירה

I need a job.
Ani tzariich avoda.
.אני צריך עבודה
She is the secretary of the company.
Hee ha mazkira shel ha chevra.
.היא המזכירה של החברה
The manager needs to hire another employee.
Ha menahel tzarich liskor oved acher.
המנהל צריך לשכור עובד אחר.
I am lucky because I have an interview for a cashier position today.
Lemazali (it's my good luck) yesh li rea'ayon bishvil misrat ha koopa'iit hayom.
.למזלי יש לי ראיון בשביל משרת קופאית היום
How much is the salary and does it include benefits?
Ma hu ha sachar ve haiim hu kolel (include) hatavot?
מה הוא השכר והאם הוא כולל הטבות?

An interview - Re'ayon - ראיון
Resumé - Korot hachayiim – קורות חיים
Presentation - Matzeg'et - מצגת
Specialist – Mumchei - מומחה
To hire – Lis'kor - לשכור
To fire – Lefater - לפטר
Pay check – Maskoret - משכורת
Income - Hachnasa - הכנסה
Salary – Sachar - שכר
Insurance – Bitooach - ביטוח
Benefits – Hatavot - הטבות
Trimester - Shlish - שליש
Budget – Taktziv - תקציב
Net – Neto - נטו
Gross – Bruto - ברוטו
To retire – Lifrosh - לפרוש
Pension - Pensiya - פנסיה
Pension - Gimlona'oot - גמלאות

I am at work at the factory now.
Ani ba avoda ba beit ha charoshet hayom.
אני בעבודה בבית החרושת היום.
In business, you should be professional.
Be asakiim ata tzarich lei'yot miktzohee.
בעסקים אתה צריך להיות מקצועי.
Is the presentation ready?
Haiim ha matzeg'et moochana (ready)?
האם המצגת מוכנה?
The first trimester is part of the annual budget.
Ha shlish ha rishon hu chelek (part) mei hataktziiv ha shnati (annual).
השליש הראשון הוא חלק מהתקציב השנתי.
I have to see the net and gross profits of the business.
Ani tzarich lir'ott et ha revach ha neto ve ha bruto shel ha esek.
אני צריך לראות את הרווח הנטו והברטו של העסק.
I want to retire already.
Ani rotzei/rotza kvar (already) lifrosh.
אני רוֹצֶה\רוֹצָה כבר לפרוש.

Client – Lakohach - לקוח
Client – (f) Lekocha - לקוחה
Broker – Metavech - מתווך
Broker – (f) Metavechet - מתווכת
Broker - Sochen סוכן / **Broker -** (f) Sochenet סוכנת
Salesperson – Zaban - זבן / **Salesperson –** (f) Zabaniit - זבנית
Salesperson – Moocher - מוכר / **Salesperson –** (f) Mocheret - מוכרת
Realtor - Metavech dir'ot – מתווך דירות
Realtor - (f) Metavachat dir'ot- מתווכת דירות
Realtor - Nadlan - נדלן / **Realtor -** (f) Nadlaniit - נדלנית
Real Estate Market - Shook ha nadlan – שוק הנדל"ן
A purchase – Rechisha - רכישה
To invest - Lehashkiya - להשקיע
Investment - Hashkaha - השקעה
Investor - Ha mashkiya - המשקיע

I can earn a huge profit from stocks.
Ani yachol lahasot revach atzoom (huge) mei ha menayot.
אני יכול לעשות רווח עצום מהמניות.

The demand in the real estate market depends on the country's economy.
Ha bikoosh ba shook ha nadlan talooy (depends) ba kalkalat ha medina.
הביקוש בשוק הנדל"ן תלוי בכלכלת המדינה.

If you want to sell your home, I can recommend a very good realtor.
Iim ata rotzei limkor et ha bait shelcha, ani yachol lahamlitz hal metavech tov me'od.
אם אתה רוצה למכור את הבית שלך, אני יכול להמליץ על מתווך טוב מאוד.

The investor wants to invest in this shopping center because of its good potential.
Hamashkiya rotzei lehashkiya bemerkaz ha kniyot hazei mikevan shei yesh potensyal gadol.
המשקיע רוצה להשקיע במרכז הקניות הזה מכיוון שיש פוטנציאל גדול.

The value of the property increased by twenty percent.
Ha erech shel ha neches ala (increased) bei esreem achooz.
הערך של הנכס עלה בעשרים אחוז.

How much is the commission on the sale?
Ma hee ha amla shel ha mechira?
מה היא העמלה של המכירה?

A lease - Chozei sechiroot – חוזי שכירות
To lease – Lehaskir - להשכיר
Landlord - Ba'al ha bait – בעל הבית
Landlord - (f) Ba'alat ha bait – בעלת הבית
Tenant – Dayar - דייר / **Tenant – (f)** Dayeret - דיירת
Mortgage - Mashkanta – משכנתא
Interest rate – Ribiit - ריבית
A loan - Alva'ha – הלוואה
Commission - Am'la - עמלה
Percent – Achooz - אחוז
Economy – Kalkala - כלכלה
A sale - Mechira - מכירה
Profit – Revach - רווח
Value – Erech - ערך
The demand - Ha bikoosh - הביקוש / **The supply -** Ha hai'tzaa - ההיצע
A contract – Chozae - חוזה
Terms - Tna'iim - תנאים
Signature – Chatima - חתימה / **Initials -** Rashei-tevot – ראשי תיבות
Stock - Mena'ya – מנייה / **Stocks -** Mena'yot – מניות
Stock broker - Metavech mena'yot – מתווך מניות
Stock broker - Sochen menayot סוכן מניות

The client wants to lease instead of purchasing the property.
Ha lakohach rotzei lehaskiir bimkom lirkosh et ha neches.
הלקוח רוצה לשכור במקום לרכוש את הנכס.

What are the terms of the purchase?
Ma hem ha tnaiim shel ha rechisha?
מה הם התנאים של הרכישה?

I can negotiate a better interest rate.
Ani yachol lenahel masa-hu-matan (negotiation) al ribit tova yoter.
אני יכול לנהל משא ומתן על ריבית טובה יותר.

I need a small loan in order to pay my mortgage this month.
Ani tzarich al'va'ha ktana kedi leshalem et ha mashkanta sheli kol chodesh.
אני צריך הלוואה כדי לשלם את המשכנתא שלי כל חודש.

I need a signature and initials on the contract.
Ani tzarich/tzreicha chatiima ve et rashei ha tevot al ha chozae.
אני צריך\צריכה חתימה ואת ראשי התיבות של החוזה.

Money - Kesef כסף
Money - Mamon ממון
Currency - Matbe'a - מטבע
Credit – Ashrai - אשראי
Cash – Mezuman - מזומן
Coins – Matbehot - מטבעות
Change (change for a bill) – Odef - עודף
Tax - Mas מס
Tax - (p) Missiim – מיסים
Price – Mechir - מחיר
Invoice – Cheshboniit - חשבונית
Receipt - Kabala קבלה
Inventory – Mlayee - מלאי
Merchandise - Secho'ra - סחורה
A refund - Echzer kaspi – החזר כספי
Product – Mutzar - מוצר
Produced – Meyutzar - מיוצר
Imports - Yevo'ha - יבוא
Exports - Yetzu'ha - יצוא

Don't forget to bring cash with you.
Al tishkach lehavi mezuman itcha.
אל תשכח להביא מזומן איתך.
Do you have change for a 100 shekel bill?
Yesh lecha/lach odef leshtar shel me'aa shekel?
יש לךָ\לָך עודף לשטר של מאה שקל?
I don't have a credit card.
Ein li kartis ashrai.
אין לי אשראי.
The salesperson told me there is no refund.
Ha mocher amar shae-ein efsharoot (possibility) le echzer.
המוכר אמר שאין אפשרות להחזר.
This product is produced in Italy.
Ha mutzar hazei hu totzeret italya.
המוצר הזה הוא תוצרת איטליה.
I work in the export/import business.
Ani oved ba tchoom (line of expertise) shel yetzoo ve yevoo.
אני עובד בתחום של יצוא ויבוא.

Retail - Kim'ona'oot - קמעונאות
Wholesale – Sitoonoot - סיטונאות
To ship – Lishloach - לשלוח
Shipment – Hovala - הובלה
Advertisement - Pirsoom פרסום
Advertisement - Pirsomet – פרסומת
Ads - Moda'hott - מודעות
To advertise – Lefarsem - לפרסם

Let me check my inventory.
Ten-li (allow me) livdok et ha mlayee sheli.
תן לי לבדוק את המלאי שלי.
This product is insured.
Ha mutzar hazei mevootach.
המוצר הזה מבוטח.
This invoice contains a mistake.
Ba cheshbonoot hazot yesh tahoot.
בחשבונית הזאת יש טעות.
What is the wholesale and retail value of this shipment?
Ma hu ha erech ha sitoni ve ha kimona'ee shel ha mishloach hazei?
מה הוא הערך הסיטוני והקמעוני של המשלוח הזה?
You don't have enough money to purchase the merchandise.
Ein lecha/lach maspiik (enough) kesef lirchosh et ha schora.
אין לךָ\לָךְ מספיק כסף לרכוש את הסחורה.
How much does the shipping cost and is it in foreign currency?
Kama olei ha mishloach ve ha'iim hu be matbeiha zaar (foreign)?
כמה עולה מישלוח והאם הוא במטבע זר?
There is a tax exemption on this income.
Yesh ptor (exemption) mei mas ha achnasa ha zae.
יש פטור ממס ההכנסה הזה.
My position in the company is marketing and I am responsible for advertising and ads.
Tafkidi ba chevra ha zot hoo shivook (marketing) ve achrayoot al ha pirsoom ve moda'hott.
תפקידי בחברה הזאת הוא שיווק ואחריות על הפרסום ומודעות.

SPORTS – SPORT - ספורט

Basketball - Kadoor sal - כדורסל
Soccer - Kadoor reg'el - כדורגל
Game – Mischak - משחק
Stadium - Iitz'tadyon - איצטדיון
Ball – Kadoor - כדור
Player – Sachkan - שחקן
Player – (f) Sachkaniit - שחקנית
To jump – Likfotz - לקפוץ
To throw – Lizrok - לזרוק
To kick – Livhot - לבעוט
To catch – Litfos - לתפוס
Coach - Mae'amen - מאמן
Coach - (f) Mae'amenet - מאמנת
Referee – Shofet - שופט
Competition – Tacharoot - תחרות
Fans – Meharitziim - מעריצים
Team - Nivcheret נבחרת
Team - Kvootza – קבוצה
Teammate - Chaver ba kvootza – חבר בקבוצה
National team - Kvootza lehoomiit – קבוצה לאומית

I like to watch basketball games.
Ani neiheinei (enjoy) litzpot bae mischak ha kadoor sal.
אני נהנה לצפות במשחק הכדורסל.
To play basketball, you need to be good at throwing and jumping.
Kedei lesachek kadoor sal ata tzarich lizrok ve likfotz ai'tev.
כדי לשחק כדורסל אתה צריך לזרוק ולקפוץ היטב.
The national team has a lot of fans.
Ba nivcheret yesh arbei ma'aritziim.
בנבחרת יש הרבה מעריצים.
My teammate can't find his helmet.
Chaver ha kvootza eino yachol limtzo et ha casda shelo.
חבר הקבוצה אינו יכול למצוא את הקסדה שלו.
The coach and the team were on the field during half-time.
Ha me'amen ve ha nivcheret hayu al ha migrash bae machatzit ha zman.
המאמן והנבחרת היו על המגרש במחצית הזמן.

Opponent - Mitnag'ed - מתנגד
Half time - Chatzi ha zman – חצי הזמן
Finals - Ha gmar - הגמר
Scores – Totzahott - תוצאות
The goal - Ha shahar - השער
A goal – Matara - מטרה
To lose - Lehafsiid - להפסיד
A Defeat - Efsed – הפסד
To win – Lenatzeiach - לנצח
A victory – Nitzachon - ניצחון
The looser - Ha mafseed - המפסיד
The winner - Ha mena'tzei'ach - המנצח
Field – Migrash - מגרש
Helmet – Casda - קסדה
A whistle – Mashrokeet - משרוקית
Penalty – Onesh - עונש
Basket – Sal - סל

Soccer is my favorite sport.
Kadoor reg'el ze ha sport ha hahoov alai beyoter (the most).
כדורגל זה הספורט האהוב עליי ביותר.
The coach needs to bring his team today to meet the new referee.
Ha me'amen tzarich lahavi et ha kvootza shelo hayom lifgosh et ha shofet ha chadash.
המאמן צריך להביא את הקבוצה שלו היום לפגוש את השופט החדש.
Our opponents went home after their defeat.
Ha yeriviim shelanu chazru habayta achrei ha tvoosa (defeat) shelahem.
היריבים שלנו חזרו הביתה אחרי התבוסה שלהם.
I have tickets to a soccer game at the stadium.
Yesh li kartisiim la mischak kadoor-reg'el ba itztadyon.
יש לי כרטיסים למשחק כדורגל באיצטדיון.
The player received a penalty for kicking the ball in the wrong goal.
Ha sachkan kibel "pendal" al be'itat ha kadoor la sha'ar ha lo-nachon (wrong).
השחקן קיבל פנדל על העיטת הכדור לשער הלא נכון.
Not every person likes sports.
Lo kol adam ohev sport.
לא כל אדם אוהב ספורט.

Athlete - Atlet - אתלט
Athlete - (f) Atlet'iit - אתלטית
Olympics - Olimpi'yada - אולימפיאדה
World cup - Sha'ar olami - שער עולמי
World cup - Gavi'a olami - גביע עולמי
Bicycle – Ofanaiim - אופניים
Cyclist - Rochev ofaniim – רוכב אופניים
Wrestling – Itavkoot - התאבקות
Boxing – Iigroof - איגרוף
Martial arts - Omanoo'yot ha lechima – אומניות הלחימה
Championship – Alifoot - אליפות
Award – Prass - פרס
Trophy - Gavee'a - גביע
Tournament – Tacharoot - תחרות
Horse racing - Merootz soosiim – מרוץ סוסים
Racing – Merootz - מרוץ
Ice skating - Gleesha al ha kerach – גלישה על הקרח
Swimming - Schee'ya - שחייה

Today are the finals for the Olympic Games.
Hayom, hoo yom hagmar shel mischakei ha olympiyada.
היום, הוא יום הגמר של משחקי האולימפיאדה.
Let's see who wins the World Cup.
Bo'hoo nerei mi yenatzei'ach begaviya ha olam.
בואו נראה מי ינצח בגביע העולם.
I want to compete in the cycling championship.
Ani rotzei/rotza lehitcharot bei-tacharoot ha ofanaiim.
אני רוֹצֶה\רוֹצָה להתחרות בתחרות האופניים.
I am an athlete so I must stay in shape.
Ani atlet/atlet'iit lachen ani tzariich/tzreicha lee'hyott be kosheir.
אני אתלט\אתלטית לכן אני צריך\צריכה להיות בכושר.
After my boxing lesson, I want to go and swim in the pool.
Achrei shioor ha igroof sheli, ani rotze/rotza lischot ba breicha.
אחרי שיעור האיגרוף שלי, אני רוֹצֶה\רוֹצָה לזכות בבריכה.
He will receive an award, he is the winner of the martial-arts tournament.
Hoo yekabel et ha prass ki hoo zacha bei tacharoot shel omaniyot ha lechima.
הוא יקבל את הפרס כי הוא זכה בתחרות של אומניות הלחימה.

Exercise - Hita'amloot - התעמלות
Exercise - pei'loot goofaneet - פעילות גופנית
A match - Mischak - משחק
Fitness - Ko'sheir goofani – כושר גופני
Gym - Cheder ko'sheir חדר כושר / **Gym** - Chadar hita'mloot חדר העתמלות
Captain - Captain קפטן / **Captain** - Rosh ha kvootza ראש הקבוצה
Judge – Shofet - שופט / **Judge** – (f) Shofetet - שופטת
Rules – Chookiim - חוקים
Track – Maslool - מסלול
Trainer - Me'amen - מאמן / **Trainer** - (f) Me'amenet - מאמנת
Pool (billiards) - Bil'yard - ביליארד
Pool (swimming pool) – Breicha - בריכה

The wrestling captain must teach his team the rules of the game.
Rosh kvootza ha itavkoot chayav leleamed et ha nivcheret et klaleyi ha mischak.
ראש קבוצת התאבקות חייב ללמד את הנחברת את כללי המשחק.

At the horse-racing competition, the judge couldn't announce the score.
Ba tacharoot ha soos'eem ha shofet lo yachol haya leho'diya et ha totza'ot.
בתחרות הסוסים השופט לא יכול היה להודיע את התוצאות.

There is a bicycle race at the park today.
Yesh tacharoot ofaniim hayom ba park.
יש תחרות אופניים היום בפארק.

This fitness program is expensive.
Tochnit ha kosheir hazot hee yekara.
תוכנית הכושר הזאת היא יקרה.

It's healthy to go to the gym every day.
Ze bari (healthy) lalechet la chadar ko'sheir kol yom.
זה בריא ללכת לחדר כושר כל יום.

Weightlifting is good exercise.
Haramat mishkolot zo pehiloot gofaniit tova.
הרמת משקולות זו פעליות גופנית טובה.

I want to run on the track today.
Ani rotzei/rotza larootz ba maslool hayom.
אני רוֹצָה\רוֹצָה לרוץ במסלול היום.

OUTDOOR ACTIVITIES - PEI'LOOT CHOOTZ – פעילות חוץ

A camp – Machanei - מחנה
Campground - Atar machnahoot – אתר מחנאות
Tent – O'hel - אוהל
RV – Caravan - קרוואן
Campfire – Medura - מדורה
Matches – Gafrooriim - גפרורים
Lighter – Matzit - מצית
Coal – Pecham - פחם
Flame – Lehava - להבה
The smoke - Ha a'ashan - העשן
Compass – Matzpen - מצפן
Camping – Machnahoot - מחנאות

There aren't any tents at the campground.
Ein o'hal'eem ba machanei.
אין אוהלים במחנה.

I want to sleep in an RV instead of a tent.
Ani rotzei/rotza lishon ba caravan bimkom ba o'hel.
אני רוֹצֶה\רוֹצָה לישון בקרוואן במקום באוהל.

We can use a lighter to start a campfire.
Anu yecholim lehishtamesh ba matzit kedei lahadlik et ha medura.
אנו יכולים להשתמש במצית כדי להדליק את המדורה.

We need coal and matches for the trip.
Anu tzreichim pecham ve gafrooriim bishvil tiyool.
אנו צריכים פחם וגפרורים בשביל הטיול.

Put out the fire because the flames are very high and there is a lot of smoke.
Techabei et ha esh ki ha lehavot me'od gvo'hott ve yesh arbei a'ashan.
תכבי את האש כי הלהבות מאוד גבוהות ויש הרבה עשן.

There is fog outside and the temperature is below freezing.
Yesh arafel bachootz ve mezeg-ha-aviir (temperature) mitachat (below) la keepa'on.
יש ערפל בחוץ ומזג אוויר מתחת לקיפאון.

Fishing - Da'eeg - דייג
To fish – Ladoog - לדוג
Hiking - Tiyool ragl'ee – טיול רגלי
Hiking trail - Shviil halicha – שבילי הליכה
Pocket knife - O'lar - אולר
Fishing pole – Chaka - חכה
Fishing line - Choot da'eeg - חוט דייג
Hook – Keres - קרס
Bait - Pita'yonn - פתיון
A float - Matz'of - מצוף
A weight - Mishkolet - משקולת
Fishing net – Reseht - רשת
To hunt - Latzood - לצוד
Rifle – Rovei - רובה

Where is the fishing store? I need to buy hooks, fishing line, bait, and a net.
Eichan chanoot ha da'eeg? Ani tzarich liknot krasiim, choot da'iig, pita'yon, ve reshet.
היכן חנות הדייג? אני צריך לקנות קרסים, חוט דייג, פיתיון ורשת.

You can't bring your fishing pole or your hunting rifle to the campground of the State Park because there is a sign there which says, "No fishing and no hunting."
Ata lo yachol lehavi et ha chaka ve et ha rovei shelcha la gan ha le'oomi ki yesh shelet (a sign) ha omer asoor (forbidden) ladoog ve asoor latzood".
אתה לא יכול להביא את החכה ואת הרובה שלך לגן הלאומי כי יש שלט שאומר ש"אסור לדוג ואסור לצוד".

I enjoy hiking on the trail, with my compass and my pocketknife.
Ani neh'enei letayel bashvil eem ha matzpen ve ha olar sheli.
אני נהנה לטייל בשביל עם המצפן והאולר שלי.

Don't forget the water bottle in your backpack.
Al tishkach lehavi et bakbook (bottle) hamaiim ba tarmil shelcha.
אל תשכח להביא את בקבוק המים בתרמיל שלך.

Sailing - Sha'eet - שייט
A sail – Mifras - מפרש
Sailboat - Siraat mifras סירת מפרש
Sailboat - Mifrasiit - מפרשית
Rowing – Chateera - חתירה
A paddle - Mash'ot - משוט
Motor - Mano'aa - מנוע
Canoe – Canoo - קאנו
Kayak – Kayac - קייאק
Rock climbing - Tipoos hariim – טיפוס הרים
Horseback riding - Rechivat soosiim – רכיבת סוסים

With a broken motor, we need a paddle to row the boat.
Eem mano'aa shavoor anu tzreichim lehishtamesh ba mashot kedei lahasheet et ha seera.
עם מנוע שבור אנו צריכים להשתמש במשוט כדי להשיט את הסירה.

It's important to know how to use a sail before sailing on a sailboat.
Chashoov ladahat eiich lehishtamesh ba mifras lifnei shayeet ba siraat-mifras.
חשוב לדעת איך להשתמש במפרש לפני שייט בסירת מפרש.

In my opinion, a kayak is much more fun than a canoe.
Leda'ati kayac yoter na'eem mi canoo.
לדעתי קייאק יותר נעים מקאנו.

There are several outdoor activities here including rock climbing and horseback riding.
Yesh kan kama pei'looyot chootz kolel tipoos hariim ve rechivat soosiim.
יש כאן כמה פעילויות חוץ כולל טיפוס הרים ורכיבת סוסים.

Diver - Tzolel - צולל
Diver - (f) Tzolelet - צוללת
Scuba diving – Tzlila - צלילה
Skydiving - Tznicha chofsheet – צניחה חופשית
Parachute - Mitznach - מצנח
Paragliding - Mitznachei rechifa – מיצנחי רחיפה
Hot air balloon - Balon poreiach – בלון פורח
Kite – Afifon - עפיפון
Surfing – Glisha - גלישה
Surf board – Galshan - גלשן
Ice skating - Gleesha al ha kerach – גלישה על הקרח
Skiing – Skee - סקי

Do I need to bring my scuba certification in order to scuba dive at the coral reef?
Haiim ani tzarich lehavi et mismachei ha tzlila kedei litzlol ba shooneet ha almog'eem?
?האם אני צריך להביא את מסמכי הצלילה כדי לצלול בשונית האלמוגים

I have my mask, snorkel, and fins.
Yesh li mashecha, snorkel, ve snapir'eem.
יש לי מסיכה, שנורקל וסנפירים.

I don't know which is scarier, sky diving or paragliding.
Ani lo yodei'a ma yoter mafcheed (scary), tznicha chofsheet o mitznachei recheefa.
אני לא יודע מה יותר מפחיד, צניחה חופשית או מיצנחי רחיפה.

My dream was always to fly in a hot-air balloon.
Ha chalom (dream) sheli tamiid haya lerachef bei balon porei'ach.
החלום שלי תמיד היה לרחף בבלון פורח.

We are going skiing on our next vacation.
Ba choofsha haba'a anachnu olcheem leskee.
בחופשה הבאה אנחנו הולכים לסקי.

Where is the surfboard? I want to surf the waves at the beach.
Eifo ha galshan? Ani rotzei liglosh al ha galeem (waves) bechof ha yam.
איפה הגלשן? אני רוצה לגלוש על הגלים בחוף הים.

Ice skating is fun.
Gleesha al kerach ze mehanei (fun) me'od.
גלישה על הקרח זה מהנה מאוד.

ELECTRICAL DEVICES
MACH'SHEE'REY CHASHMAL – מכשירי חשמל

Electricity – Chashmal - חשמל
Appliance – Machsheer - מכשיר
Oven – Tanoor - תנור
Stove – Keerayeem - כיריים
Microwave – Microgal - מיקרוגל
Refrigerator – Mekarer - מקרר
Freezer – Makpee - מקפיא
Alarm - Haza'aka - אזעקה
Smoke detector - Galai ashan – גלאי עשן

He needs to pay his electric bill if he wants electricity.
Hoo tzarich leshalem et cheshbon ha chashmal shelo eem hoo rotzae aspakat chashmal.
הוא צריך לשלם את חשבון החשמל שלו אם הוא רוצה אספקת חשמל.

I want to purchase a few things at the electronic appliance store.
Ani rotzei/rotza liknot kama dvariim ba chanoot le machsherey chashmal.
אני רוֹצֶה\רוֹצָה לקנות כמה דברים בחנות למכשירי חשמל.

I can't put plastic utensils in the dishwasher.
Ani lo yachol lahachnis kelei plastic la madiach ha keleem.
אני לא יכול להכניס כלי פלסטיק למדיח כלים.

I am going to get rid of my microwave and oven because they are not functioning.
Ani niftar (get rid) mi ha mikrogal ve ha tanoor sheli kee hem lo pei'leem.
אני נפטר מהמיקרוגל והתנור שלי כי הם לא פועלים.

The refrigerator and freezer aren't cold enough.
Ha mekarer ve ha hakpa'a lo maspeek kaar'eem.
המקרר וההקפאה לא מספיק קרים.

Is that annoying sound the alarm clock or the fire alarm?
Haiim ha rahash (noise) ha ma'atzben hazei hoo min ha shao'n ha me'orer o azakat esh.
האם הרעש המעצבן הזה הוא מין השעון המעורר או אזעקת אש.

Coffee maker - Mechonat kafae – מכונת קפה
Coffee pot- Kankan kafae – קנקן קפה
Toaster – Toster - טוסטר
Dishwasher - Madiach keleem – מדיח כלים
Laundry machine - Mechonat kveesa – מכונת כביסה
Laundry – Kveesa - כביסה
Dryer - Mechonat yeboosh- מכונת יבוש
Fan - Mae'avrer - מאוורר
Air condition – Mazgan - מזגן
Remote control - Shlat rachok- שלט רחוק
Battery – Solela - סוללה

The coffee maker and toaster are in the kitchen.
Mechonat ha kafei ve ha toster hem ba mitbach.
מכונת הקפה והטוסטר הם במטבח.

My washing machine and dryer do not function therefore I must wash my laundry at the public laundromat.
Mechonat ha kvisa sheli ve ha meyabesh einam-pei'leem (they don't function) lachen ani tzarich lechabes et ha kveesa sheli ba londromat ha tzibooree (public).
מכונת הכביסה שלי והמייבש אינם פועלים לכן אני צריך לכבס את הכביסה שלי בלונדרומאט הציבורי.

Is this fan new?
Ha'iim ha me'avrer ha zei chadash?
האם המאוורר הזה חדש?

Unfortunately, the new air conditioner unit hasn't been delivered yet.
Letza'ari (unfortunately) yechidat (unit) ha mazgan ha chadasha terem nimsera (delivered).
לצערי יחידת המזגן החדשה טרם נמסרה.

The smoke detector needs new batteries.
Gala'yee ha a'shan zakook le solelot chadashot.
גלאי העשן זקוק לסוללות חדשות.

Lamp – Menora - מנורה
Light bulb – Noora - נורה
A (wall) clock - Orlog'een - אורלוגין
A watch - Sha'on - שעון
Vacuum cleaner - Sho'ev avak – שואב אבק
Phone - Teléfon - טלפון
Text message - Hoda'at mesiron – הודעת מסרון
Voice message - Hoda'a-koleet – הודעה קולית
Camera – Matzlema - מצלמה

The clock is hanging on the wall.
Ha sha'on taloo'yee (hanging) al a keer.
השעון תלוי על הקיר.

The cordless stereo is on the table.
Ha stereo ha al-choot'ee (cordless) al ha shoolchan.
הסטריאו האלחוטי על השולחן.

I still have a home telephone.
Ada'een yesh li telephon beiti.
עדיין יש לי טלפון ביתי.

I need to buy a lamp and a vacuum cleaner today.
Ani tzarich/tzreicha liknot menora ve sho'ev avak ayom.
אני צריך\צריכה לקנות מנורה ושואב אבק היום.

In the past, cameras were more common. Today, everyone can use their phones to take pictures.
Ba'avar (in the past) ha matzlemot hayu yoter (more) nefotzot (common). Ayom koolam mishtamshim ba telephon'eem shelahem kedei letzalem.
בעבר המצלמות היו יותר נפוצות. היום כולם משתמשים בטלפונים שלהם כדי לצלם.

You can leave me a voice message or send me a text message.
Ata yachol lehasheer li hodaa'a koleet o lishloach hoda'at misron.
אתה יכול להשאיר לי הודעה קולית או לשלוח הודעת מסרון.

Flashlight – Panas - פנס
Light – Orr - אור
Furnace – Kivshan - כבשן
Heater - Ha'meseek - מסיק
Cord – Cabel - כבל
Charger - Mat'enn - מטען
Outlet - Sheka'a - שקע
Headsets - Oz'niyot - אוזניות
Doorbell - Pa'aamon ha delet – פעמון הדלת
Lawn mower - Mekasei'ach de'shaei – מכסחת דשא

The lights don't function when there is a blackout therefore I must rely on my flashlight.
Ha orot einam po-a'a-leem ke'shei yesh afsakat chashmal ve lachen ani chayav/chayevet leestamech (to rely) ba panas sheli.
האורות אינם פועלים כשיש הפסקת חשמל ולכן אני חייב\חיבת להשתמש בפנס שלי.

I can't hear the doorbell.
Ani lo yachol/yachola lishmoa'a et pa'aamon ha delet.
אני לא יכול\יכולה לשמוע את פעמון הדלת.

There is a higher risk of causing a house fire from an electric heater than a furnace.
Yesh sikoon (risk) gavo'a (higher) yoter (more) ligrom sreifat ba'it beshimoosh (with the use of) meseek chashmali ma'asher ha kivshan.
יש סיכון גבוה יותר לגרום שריפת בית בשימוש מסיק חשמלי מאשר הכבשן.

I need to connect the cord to the outlet.
Ani tzarich/tzreicha lechaber et ha cabel la sheka'a.
Mekasachat ha deshaei shelo mara'aeesh (noisy) me'od.
אני צריך\צריכה לחבר את הכבל לשקע. מכסחת הדשא שלו מרעישה מאוד.

Why is my headset on the floor?
Mado'a ha oz'ni'yot sheli al ha ritzpa (floor)?
מדוע האוזניות שלי על הריצפה?

TOOLS – KLEI AVODA – כלי עבודה

Toolbox - Argaz kel'eem – ארגז כלים
Carpenter – Nagar - נגר
Hammer - Patt'eesh - פטיש
Saw - Mas'or - מסור
Axe – Garzen - גרזן
A drill - Makdecha – מקדחה
To drill - Lik'doe'ach - לקדוח
Nail - Masmer - מסמר
A screw - Bo'reg - בורג
Screwdriver - Mavreg - מברג
A wrench - Maftei'ach brag'eem – מפתח ברגים
Pliers - Melka'cha'yeem - מלקחיים
Ladder - Soo'lam - סולם
Rope – Chevel - חבל
String – Choot -חוט
A scale - Mozna'yeem - מאזניים
To paint - Litzboa'a - לצבוע
The paint – Tzeva - צבע

The carpenter needs nails, a hammer, a saw, and a drill.
Ha nagar zakook le masmer'eem, patish, masor, ve makdecha.
הנגר זקוק למסמרים, פטיש, מסור ומקדחה.
The string is very long. Where are the scissors?
Ha choot me'od aroch (long). Eifo ha mispara'eem?
החוט מאוד ארוך. איפה המספריים?
The screwdriver is in the toolbox.
Ha mavreg nimtza ba argaz kel'eem.
המברג נמצא בארגז כלים.
This tool can cut through metal.
Ha kl'ee ha zei yachol lachatoch matechet.
הכלי הזה יכול לחתוך מתכת.
The ladder is next to the tools.
Ha soo'lam leyad ha kel'eem.
הסולם ליד הכלים.

Paint brush – Mivreshet - מברשת
Measuring tape - Seret medida – סרט מדידה
Machine – Mechona - מכונה
A lock - Mano'ol - מנעול / **Locked** - Nao'ol - נעול
To lock - Lino'ol - לנעול
Equipment - Tzi'yood - ציוד
Metal - Matechet - מתכת
Steel – Plada - פלדה
Iron – Barzel - ברזל
Broom - Mata'tei - מטאטא
Dust pan - Ya'eh - יאה
Mop – Magav - מגב / **Mop** - Smartoot ritzpa - סמרטוט ריצפה
Bucket - Dl'ee - דלי
Sponge – Sfog - ספוג
Shovel - Ett - את
A trowel - Kaaf chafeera – כף חפירה

I must buy a brush to paint the walls.
Alai liknot mivreshet litzbo'a et ha kirot.
עליי לקנות מברשצ לצבוע את הקירות.
The paint bucket is empty.
Dl'ee ha tzeva reik (empty).
דלי הצביעה ריק.
It's better to tie the shovel with a rope in my pick up truck.
A'dif likshor et ett ha chafira bei chevel ba tender sheli.
עדיף לקשור את החפירה בחבל בטנדר שלי.
How can I fix this machine?
Keitzad ochal letaken et ha mechona ha zot?
כיצד אוכל לתקן את המכונה הזאת?
The broom and dust pan are with the rest of my cleaning equipment.
Ha mata'tei ve ha ya'eh nimtza'eem bei-shei'ar (with the rest) ha tziyood (equipment) sheli.
המטאטא והיאה נמצאים עם שאר הציוד שלי.
Where did you put the mop and the bucket?
Eifo samta et ha magav ve ha dl'ee?
איפה שמת את המגב והדלי?

CAR - OTO - אוטו
CAR - RECHEV - רכב
CAR - MECHONEET - מכונית

Engine - Mano'a - מנוע / **Ignition** – Hatzata - הצתה
Automatic – Automati - אוטומטי / **Manual** – Yadani - ידני
Gear shift – Heeloochim - הילוכים
Seat – Moshav - מושב
Seat belt - Chagorat beetachon – חגורת ביטחון
Brakes – Balameem - בלמים
Handbrake - Balam yadani – בלם ידני
Airbag - Kareet aviir – כרית אוויר

I must take my car to my mechanic because there is a problem with the ignition.
Alai lakachat et ha mechonit sheli la mechona'ee kee yesh baa'aya (problem) eem ha atzata.
עליי לקחת את המכונית שלי למכונאי כי יש בעיה עם ההצתה.

What happened to the engine?
Ma kara la mano'a?
מה קרה למנוע?

The seat is missing a seat belt.
Bamoshav chasera (missing) chagorat bitachon.
במושב חסרה חגורת בטיחות.

I prefer a gear shift instead of an automatic car.
Ani mahadeef heeloocheem bimkom oto otomatee.
אני מעדיף הילוכים במקום אוטו אוטומטי.

The brakes are new in this vehicle
Ha balameem hem chadasheem ba rechev ha zei.
הבלמים הם חדשים ברכב הזה.

This vehicle doesn't have a handbrake.
Larechev hazei ein balam yadani.
לרכב הזה אין בלם ידני.

There is an airbag on both the driver side and the passenger side.
Yesh kareet avir gam betzad ha nahag ve gam betzad ha noseia'a.
יש כרית אוויר גם בצד הנהג וגם בצד הנוסע.

My car doesn't have an alarm.
Een aza'aka ba mechonit sheli.
אין אזעקה במכונית שלי.

Steering wheel - Hei'gae - הגה
Driver seat - Moshav ha na'hagg – מושב לנהג
Passenger seat - Moshav ha noseia'a – מושב הנוסע
Front seat - Moshav kidmee – מושב קדמי
Back seat - Moshav achoree – מושב אחורי
Car passenger - Nosei'a ha rechev – נוסעי הרכב
Baby seat - Moshav la tinokot – מושב לתינוקות
Baby seat - Kee'say la tinok – מושב לתינוק
Warning light - Noorat hazhara – נורת אזהרה
Horn (of the car) – Tzoofar - צופר
Button - Kaftor - כפתור
Windshield - Shmasha kidmeet – שמשה קידמית
Windshield wiper – Magav - מגב
Windshield fluid - Nozel shmashot – נוזל שמשות
Rear view mirror - Re'ee achoree ראי אחורי
Rear view mirror - Mar'a achoreet – מראה אחורית
Side mirror - Re'ee tzdad'ee ראי צד
Side mirror - Mar'a tzdad'eet – מראה צדדית
Alarm - Aza'aka - אזעקה
Window – Chalon - חלון

When driving, both hands must be on the steering wheel.
Ke shae nohag'eem shtey (both) ha yadaiim chayvoot liyot al ha hei'gae.
כשנוהגים שתי הידיים חייבות להיות על ההגה.

The baby seat is in the back seat.
Kee'say ha tinok nimtza ba moshav ha achoree.
כיסא התינוק נמצא במושב האחורי.

The warning light button is located next to the stirring wheel.
Noorat ha azhara nimtzet (located) leyad ha hei'gae.
נורת האזהרה נמצאת ליד ההגה.

The windshield and all four of my car windows are cracked.
Ha shmasha ha kidmeet ve kol arba'at ha chalonot ba rechev sheli sdook'eem (cracked).
השמשה הקדמית וכל ארבעת החלונות ברכב שלי סדוקים.

I want to clean my rear-view mirror and my side mirrors.
Ani rotzei/rotza lenakot et re'hee ha achoree sheli ve et mar'ott ha tzadadee'yot.
אני רוֹצֶה\רוֹצָה לנקות את הראי האחורי שלי ואת מראות הצדדיות.

Door handle - Yad'eet ha delet – ידית הדלת
Spare tire - Tzameeg chaloofee – צמיג רזרבי
Trunk - Taa mita'an – תא מטען
Hood (of the vehicle) - Michsei ma'no'aa – מכסה מנוע
Drive license - Rishayon ne'hee'ga – רישיון נהיגה
License plate – Tzlocheet – לוחית רישוי
Gasoline – Delek - דלק
Low fuel - Delek namooch – דלק נמוך
Flat tire - Teker - תקר
Flat tire - Pancher פנצ'ר
Crowbar – Hamot harama – המוט הרמה
A (car) jack - Mag'bee'ha - מגביהה
Wrench – Maftei'ach brag'eem – מפתח ברגים

The door handle on the driver's side doesn't function.
Yadeet ha delet bae tzad ha nahag lo po'elet.
ידית הדלת הצד הנהג לו פועלת.
Your license plate has expired.
Loocheet ha resho'ee shelcha kvar lo betokef.
לוחית הרישוי שלך כבר לא בתוקף.
I want to renew my driving license today.
Hayom ani rotzei/rotza lechadesh et rishayon ha ne'hee'ga sheli.
היום אני רוֹצֶה\רוֹצָה לחדש את רישיון הנהיגה שלי.
Are the car doors locked?
Haiim dlat'oot ha oto ne'ool'ott?
האם דלתות האוטו נעולות?
Does this car have a spare tire in the trunk?
Ha'iim yesh tzamig chaloofee (spare) ba taa ha mita'an sheli?
האם יש צמיג חלופי בתא המטען שלי?
Please, close the car door.
Bevakasha, sgor/sigrei et delet ha mechoneet.
בבקשה, סגור\סגרי את דלת המכונית.
Where is the nearest gas station?
Eifo tachanat ha delek ha krova-beyoter (the nearest)?
איפה תחנת הדלק הקרובה ביותר?
The windshield wipers are new.
Megavei ha shmasha ha kidmyeem hem chadashiim.
מגבי השמשה הקדמית הם חדשים.

NATURE - TE'VAA - טבע

A plant - Tzemach - צמח
Forest - Ya'ar - יער
Tree - Etz - עץ
Wood - Etz - עץ
Trunk - Gaeza - גזע
Branch - Anaf - ענף
Leaf - Alaei - עלה
Root - Shoresh - שורש
Flower – Peirach - פרח
Petal - A'alei ha koteret - עלי הכותרת
Blossom - Preecha - פריחה
Stem - Guivo'l - גבעול
Seed - Zera - זרע
Seed - Gar'een - גרעין

I want to collect a few leaves during the fall.
Ani rotze lehesof kama (a few) alim bae tkoofat (during/throughout) ha shalechet (fall).
אני רוצה לאסוף כמה עלים בתקופת השלכת
There aren't any plants in the desert during this season.
Ein tzmachim ba midbar bezman (during the time) ha ona hazot.
אין צמחים במדבר בזמן העונה הזאת.
The trees need rain.
Ha etziim zkookim legeshem.
העצים זקוקים לגשם.
The trunk, the branches, and the roots are all parts of the tree.
Ha geza, ha anafeem, ve ha shorashim em chelkyee ha etz.
הגזע, הענפים והשורשים הם חלקי העץ.
The orchid needs to bloom because I want to see its beautiful petals.
Ha sachlav tzarich lifroach ki ani rotzei/rotza lirot et alei ha koteret ha yafiim shelo.
הסחלב צריך לפרוח כי אני רוֹצֶה\רוֹצָה לראות את עלי הכותרת היפים שלו.
Where can I plant the seeds?
Eichan oochal lishtol et ha zra'eem?
היכן אוכל לשתול את הזרעים?

Rose - Vered - ורד
Nectar - Tzoof - צוף
Pollen - Avkaneem - אבקנים
Vegetation – Tzimchiya - צמחיה
Bush - See'ach - שיח
Grass - Deshaei - דשא
Season - Ona - עונה
Spring - Aviv - אביב
Summer - Ka'yeetz - קיץ
Winter - Choref - חורף
Autumn - Stav - סתיו
Fall - Shalechet - שלכת
Rain forest - Ya'ar geshem - יער גשם
Tropical - Tropi - טרופי
Palm tree - Etz dekel - עץ דקל

My rose bushes are beautiful.
Seechei ha vradim sheli yafeifi'eem.
שיחי הורדים שלי יפהפיים.
I must trim the grass and vegetation in my garden.
Alai lekatzetz et ha deshaei ve ha tzimchi'ya ba guina sheli.
עליי לקצץ את הדשא והצמחיה בגינה שלי.
The rain forest is a nature preserve.
Ya'aar ha geshem hoo shmorat (preserve) teva.
יער הגשם הוא שמורת טבע.
Palm trees can only grow in a tropical climate.
Atzei ha dekel yecholim litzmoach rak bae aklim (climate) tropi.
עצי הדקל יכולים לצמוח רק באקלים טרופים.
I am allergic to pollen.
Yesh li alerguia la avkaneem/Ani alergui la avkaneem.
יש לי אלרגיה לאבקנים \ אני אלרגי לאבקנים.
Is the nectar from the flower sweet?
Ha'iim tzoof ha perach matok (sweet)?
האם צוף הפרח מתוק?
Be careful because the plant stem can break very easily.
Heeza'her ki giv'ol ha tzemach yachol lehishaver me'od baekaloot (easily).
היזהר כי גבעול הצמח יכול להישבר מאוד בקלו

Sea – Yam - ים
Ocean - Okyan'oos - אוקיינוס
Waterfall - Mapal ma'eem - מפל מים
Lake – Agam - אגם
River - Nahar - נהר
Canal - Te'a'la - תעלה
Swamp - Bitza - ביצה
Mountain - Haar - הר
Hill - G'eeva'a - גבעה
Cliff - Tzook - צוק
The peak - Ha pisga - הפסגה
Rainbow - Keshet - קשת
Cloud - Anan - ענן
Lightning - Barak - ברק
Thunder - Ra'am - רעם
Rain – Geshem - גשם
Sky - Shamaiim - שמים

There is a rainbow above the waterfall.
Yesh keshet me'al la mapal.
יש קשת מעל למפל.
The ocean is bigger than the sea.
Ha okyan'oos gadol mei ha yam.
האוקיינוס גדול מהים.
From the mountain, I can see the river.
Min ha haar ani yachol lir'ot et ha nahar.
מן ההר אני יכול לראות את הנהר.
There aren't any clouds in the sky.
Ein ananeem ba shamaiim.
אין עננים בשמיים.
I see the lightning from my window.
Ani ro'ei brak'eem mi ha chalon sheli.
אני רואה ברקים מהחלון שלי.
I can hear the thunder from outside.
Ani yachol lishmo'a re'am'eem ba chootz.
אני יכול לשמוע רעמים בחוץ.

Snow – Sheleg - שלג
Ice - Keirach - קרח
Hail - Barad - ברד
Fog - A'arafel - ערפל
Wind - Roo'ach - רוח
Air - Aveer - אוויר
Dawn - Shachar - שחר
Dew - Tal - טל
Sunset - Shkee'ya - שקיעה
Sunrise - Zricha - זריחה
Deep - A'amok - עמוק
Shallow - Ra'dude - רדוד

I want to see the sunset from the hill.
Ani rotzei lir'ot et ha shki'ya mi ha giv'a.
אני רוצה לראות את השקיעה מהגבעה.
The lake has a shallow part and a deep part.
Ba agam yesh chelek ra'dude ve chelek a'amok.
באגם יש חלק רדוד וחלק עמוק.
I don't like the wind.
Ani lo ohev/ohevet et ha roo'ach.
אני לא אוהב\אוהבת את הרוח.
The air on the mountain is very clear.
Ha avir ba haar me'od tzalool (clear).
האוויר בהר מאוד צלול.
Every dawn, there is dew on the leaves of my plants.
Bechol a'loott-ha (rise of) shachar yesh tal al alei ha tzmacheem sheli.
בכל עלות השחר יש טל על עלי הצמחים שלי.
Is this ice or hail?
Haiim ze kerach o barad.
האם זה קרח או ברד.
I can see the volcano.
Ani yachol/yechola lirot et haar ha ga'ash.
אני יכול\יכולה לראות את הר הגעש.
Today we hope to see snow.
Hayom anu mekavim (we hope) lir'ot sheleg.
היום אנו מקווים לראות שלג.

World - Olam - עולם
Earth - Kadoor ha aretz - כדור הארץ
Sun - Shemesh - שמש
Moon - Yarei'ach - ירח
Crescent - Sahar - סהר
Full moon - Levana - לבנה
Star - Kochav - כוכב
Planet - Kochav lechet - כוכב לכת
Fire - Esh - אש
Heat - Cho'm - חום
Humidity - Lachoot - לחות
Island - Ee'ee - אי
Cave - Maea'ara - מערה

The moon and the stars are beautiful in the night sky.
Ha yarei'ach ve ha kochav'eem yafiim bei shmei ha laila.
הירח והכוכבים יפים בשמי הלילה.

The earth is a planet.
Kadoor ha aretz nechshav le kochav lechet.
כדור הארץ נחשב לכוכב לכת.

The heat today is unbearable.
Ha chom hayom bilti-nisbal (unbearable).
החום היום בלתי נסבל.

At the beach there is fresh air.
Bae chof ha yam yesh aviir-tzach (*tzach* - "fresh", however *tari* is "fresh" relating to foods).
בחוף הים יש אוויר צח.

I want to sail to the island to see the sunrise.
Ani rotzei/rotza lahafleeg la e'ee lir'ot et ha zreecha.
אני רוֹצָה\רוֹצָה להפליג לאי לראות את הזריחה.

We live in a beautiful world.
Anu chaeem bae olam yefei'fei.
אנו חיים בעולם יפהפייה.

Public park - Gan tziboori - גן ציבורי
National park - Gan le'oo'mee - גן לאומי
Rock - Sel'a - סלע
Stone - Ev'en - אבן
Agriculture - Chaklahoot - חקלאות
Field - Sa'deh - שדה
Ground / soil – Adama - אדמה
Weeds - Asaveem - עשבים
Sea shore - Chof ha yam - חוף הים
Seashell - Tzdafa - צדפה
Horizon – Ofek - אופק
Ray - Keren - קרן
Dry - Yavesh - יבש
Wet - Ratoov - רטוב
A stick - Makel - מקל
Dust - Avak - אבק

Parts of the cave are dry and other parts are wet.
Chelekei ha me'ara yavesh'eem ve chelak'eem acherim retoov'eem.
חלקי המערה יבשים וחלקים אחרים רטובים.
There is dust from the fire in the park.
Yesh avak mae ha esh ba gan.
יש אבק מהאש בגן.
I want to collect seashells from the seashore.
Ani rotze/rotza le'esof tzdafim al chof ha yam.
אני רוֹצֶה\רוֹצָה לאסוף צדפים על חוף הים.
There are too many stones in the soil so it's impossible to use this area as a field for agricultural purposes.
Yesh yoter midai avan'eem ba adama ve lachen ze bilti-efshari (impossible) lehishtamesh ba ezor (area) azei kee sa'deh lematarot (purposes) chakla'ee'yot.
יש יותר מידי אבנים באדמה ולכן זה בלתי אפשרי להשתמש באזור הזה כשדה למטרות חקלאיות.
Why are there so many weeds growing by the swamp?
Madoo'a yesh kol kach harbei asaveem shei tzomchim al yad ha bitza?
מדוע יש כל כך הרבה עשבים בצומחים על יד הביצה?

ANIMALS - CHAYOT חיות / BA'ALEI CHA'EEM - בעלי חיים

Pet - Chayot machmad - חיות מחמד
Mammals - Yonkeem - יונקים
Dog - Kelev - כלב
Dog - (f) Kalba - כלבה
Cat - Chatool- חתול
Cat - (f) Chatoola - חתולה
Parrot - Tookee - תוכי
Pigeon - Yona - יונה
Pig – Chazir - חזיר
Sheep - Kivsa - כבשה
Sheep - (m) Keves כבש
Cow - Par'a פרה
Bull - Shor שור
Donkey - Chamor חמור
Horse – Soos סוס
Camel - Gamal גמל

I have a dog and two cats.
Yesh li kelev ve shnei chatoolim.
יש לי כלב ושני חתולים.

There is a bird on the tree.
Yesh tzipor aa'l ha etz.
יש ציפור על העץ.

I want to go to the zoo to see the animals.
Ani rotzei/rotza lalechet la gan chayot kedey lir'ott et ba'alei ha chay'eem.
אני רוֹצֶה\רוֹצָה ללכת לגן חיות כדי לראות את בעלי החיים

My daughter wants a pet horse.
Ha bat sheli rotza soos kee chayat machmad.
הבת שלי רוצה סוס כחיית מחמד.

A pig, a sheep, a donkey, and a cow are considered farm animals.
Chazir, kivsa, chamor, huu par'a nechshav'eem ke chayot kfar.
חזיר, כבשה, חמור ופרה נחשבים כחיות כפר.

Rodent – Mecharsem מכרסם
Mouse - Achbar עכבר
Rat - Achbarosh - עכברוש
Rabbit - Shafan שפן
Hare - Arnav - ארנב
Hamster - Og'er - אוגר
Duck - Barvaz - ברווז
Goose – Avaz - אווז
Turkey - Tarnegol ho'doo - תרנגול הודו
Chicken - Tarneg'olet - תרנגולת
Rooster - Tarnegol - תרנגול
Poultry - Off - עוף
Poultry - (p) Off'ott - עופות
Squirrel - Sna'ee - סנאי

I want a hamster as a pet.
Ani rotzei/rotza og'er kee chayat machmad.
אני רוצה\רוצה אוגר כחיית מחמד.
A camel is a desert animal.
Gamal hoo chayat midbar.
גמל הוא חיית מדבר
Can I put ducks, geese, and turkeys inside my coop?
Hayeem ochal laseem barvaz'eem, avaz'eem, ve tarnegol'ayee hodoo ba lool (coop) sheli?
האם אוכל לשים ברווזים, אווזים ותרנגולות הודו בלול שלי?
We have rabbits and squirrels in our yard.
Yesh lanoo arnav'ott ve sna'eem ba chatzer (yard) shelanoo.
יש לנו ארנבות וסנאים בחצר שלנו.
It's cruel to keep a parrot inside a cage.
Ze achzari (cruel) lahachzeek tookee bei kloov (cage).
זה אכזרי להחזיק תוכי בכלוב.
There are many pigeons in the city.
Yesh harbei yon'eem ba iir.
יש הרבה יונים בעיר.
Mice and rats are rodents.
Achbar'eem ve achbarosh'eem nechsaveem (considered) le mecharsem'eem.
עכברים ועכברושים נחשבים למכרסמים.

Lion – Aryae - אריה
Hyena - Tzavo'a - צבוע
Leopard – Namer - נמר
Panther – Panter - פנתר
Cheetah - Bardales - ברדלס
Elephant – Peel - פיל
Rhinoceros – Karnaf - קרנף
Hippopotamus - Hipopotam - היפופוטם
Bat - Atalef - עטלף

There are a lot of animals in the forest.
Yesh harbei ba'alei cha'eem ba ya'ar.
יש הרבה בעלי חיים ביער.

The most dangerous animal in Africa is not the lion, it's the hippopotamus.
Ha chaya achi mesookenet bae africa hee lo ha aryae ela ha hipopotam.
החייה הכי מסוכנת באפריקה היא לא האריה אלה ההיפופוטם.

It's usually very difficult to see a leopard in the wild.
Bederech klal kashei me'od lir'ot namer ba teva.
בדרך כלל קשה מאוד לראות נמר בטבע.

Cheetahs are common in certain regions of Africa.
Bardales'eem nefotzim bae ezorim (regions) mesooyam'eem (certain) bae africa aval neder'eem (rare) bae ezoreem acherim.
ברדלסים נפוצים באזורים מסוימים באפריקה אבל נדירים באזורים אחרים.

Elephants and rhinoceroses are known as very aggressive animals.
Peel'eem ve karnaf'eem hem yedoo'eem ke chayot tok'pani'yot (aggressive) me'od.
פילים וקרנפים הם ידועים כחיות תוקפניות מאוד.

I saw a hyena and a panther at the safari yesterday.
Ra'eetee tzavo'a ve panter ba safari etmol.
ראיתי צבוע ופנתר בספארי אתמול.

Fox - Shooa'al - שועל
Wolf - Ze'ev - זאב
Weasel - Ne'mee'ya - נמייה
Otter - Lootra - לוטרה
Otter - Kel'ev nahar - כלב נהר
Bear – Dovv - דוב
Tiger - Tigris - טיגריס
Deer - Tzvi - צבי
Monkey - Koff - קוף
Monkey - (f) Kofa - קופה
Marsupial - Chayat kees - חיית כיס

A wolf is much bigger than a fox.
Ze'ev yoter gadol mi shooa'al.
זאב יותר גדול משועל.

Are there bears in this forest?
Ha'eem yesh doob'eem ba ya'ar ha'zei?
האם יש דובים ביער הזה?

Bats are the only mammals that can fly.
Atalef'eem em ha yonkim ha yechideem shae yecholim la'oof.
עטלפים הם היונקים היחידים שיכולים לעוף.

The largest member of the cat family is the tiger.
Ha tigris hu echad ha chayot ha gdoleem beyoter bae mishpachat (family) ha chatol'eem.
הטיגריס הוא אחד החיות הגדולים ביותר במשפחת החתולים.

Deer hunting is forbidden in the national park.
Tza'eed (hunting) tzva'eem asoor ba gan ha le'oomee.
צייד צבאים אסור בגן הלאומי.

There are many monkeys on the branches of the trees.
Al anfei ha etz'eem yeshnam (there are) kof'eem rab'eem.
על ענפי העצים ישנם קופים רבים.

An opossum isn't a rat but it's a marsupial just like the kangaroo.
Opasoom hoo lo achbarosh ela hoo chayat kees bidyook (exactly) kmo ha ken'gae'roo.
אופוסום הוא לא עכברוש אלה הוא חיית כיס בדיוק כמו קנגורו.

Bird - Tzi'porr - ציפור
Crow - O'rev - עורב
Stork - Chaseeda - חסידה
Vulture - Nesher - נשר
Eagle - A'eet - עייט (However, in Biblical Hebrew "eagle" is נשר - *nesher*)
Owl - Yanshoof - ינשוף
Peacock - Tavas - טווס
Reptile - Zochel - זוחל
Turtle – Tzav - צב
Snake - Nachash - נחש
Lizard - Leta'a - לטאה
Crocodile - Tan'een - תנין
Frog - Tzfardei'a - צפרדע

An eagle and an owl are birds of prey however vultures are scavengers.
A'eet ve yanshoof em off'ott dorseem aval neshar'eem em ochlei-nevelot (scavengers).
עייט וינשוף הם עופות דורסים אבל נשרים הם אוכלי-נבלות.

Crows are very smart.
Orv'eem me'od chacham'eem (smart).
עורבים מאוד חכמים.

I want to see the stork migration in Israel.
Ani rotzei/rotza lir'ot et nedidat (migration) ha chaseed'ott bae ees'ra'el.
אני רוֹצֶה/רוֹצָה לראות את נדידת החסידות בישראל.

Don't buy a fur coat!
Al tikn'ei me'il (coat) parva!
על תקני מעיל פרווה!

Butterflies and peacocks are colorful.
Parpar'eem ve tavas'eem hem tzivonee'yeem (colorful).
פרפרים וטווזים הם צבעוניים.

Some snakes are poisonous.
Chelek mei ha nachash'eem hem arsee'eem (poisonous).
חלק מהנחשים הם ארסיים.

Seal - Kelev yam - כלב ים
Whale - Livyatan - לוויתן
Dolphin - Dolfin - דולפין
Fish - Dagg - דג
Shark - Kareesh - כריש
Wing - Kanaf - כנף
Feather - Notzha - נוצה
Tail – Zanav - זנב
Fur - Parva - פרווה
Scales - Kaskas'eem - קשקשים
Fins - Snapeer'eem - סנפירים
Horns - Karna'eem - קרניים
Claws - Tefreim - טפרים

Is that the sound of a cricket or a frog?
Ha'eem ze kol ha tzar'tzar o ha tzfardei'a.
האם זה קול הצרצר או הצפרדע?

Lizards, crocodiles, and turtles belong to the reptile family.
Leta'ott, taneen'eem, ve tzaveem shayach'eem-le (belong to) mishpachat ha zochal'eem.
לטאות, תנינים וצבים שייכים למשפחת הזוחלים.

I want to see the fish in the lake.
Ani rotzei lir'ott et ha dagg ba a'gam.
אני רוצה לראות את הדג באגם.

There were a lot of seals basking on the beach last week.
Hayu harbei kalbei yam al ha chof bae shavo'a shae'avar (past).
היו הרבה כלבי ים על החוף בשבוע שעבר.

A whale is not a fish.
Livyatan hoo lo dagg.
לוויתן הוא לא דג.

Insect - Charak - חרק
A cricket - Tzar'tzar - צרצר
Ant - Nemala - נמלה
Termite - Term'eet - טרמיט
A fly – Zvoov - זבוב
Butterfly - Parpar - פרפר
Worm - Tol'a'att - תולעת
Mosquito - Yatoosh - יתוש
Flea - Par'osh - פרעוש
Lice - Keen'eem - כינים
Beetle – Chiposheet - חיפושית
A roach - Teekan - תיקן
A roach - Tjook - ג'וק
Bee – Dvora - דבורה

I want to buy mosquito spray.
Ani rotzei/rotza liknot tarsees (spray) le yatoosh'eem.
אני רוֹצֶה\רוֹצָה לקנות תרסיס ליתושים.

I need antiseptic for my bug bites.
Ani tzarich/tzreicha chitoo'ee (antiseptic) neg'ed akitzoot (bites) ha charak'eem.
אני צריך\צריכה חיטוי נגד עקיצות החרקים.

I hope there aren't any worms, ants, or flies in the bag of sugar.
Ani mekavei/mekava shae ba sac ha soocar ein tola'eem, nemal'eem, o zvoov'eem.
אני מְקַוֶּה\מְקַוָּה שבשק הסוכר אין תולעים, נמלים או זבובים.

Bees are very important for the environment.
Ha dvor'ott chashoov'ott me'od la sveeva (environment).
הדבורות חשובות מאוד לסביבה.

Beetles are my favorite insects.
Chipoosh'iyot hen ha charakeem ha chav'eev'eem (favorite) alaia?
חיפושיות הן החרקים החביבים עליה?

I need to call the exterminator because there are fleas, roaches, and termites in my house.
Ani tzarich likro la merases (exterminator) mikevan shae yesh harbei barchash'eem, teekan'eem ve termit'eem ba ba'itt sheli.
אני צריך לקרוא למרסס מכיוון שיש הרבה ברחשים, תיקנים וטרמיטים בבית שלי.

Spider - Akaveesh - עכביש
Scorpion - A'krabb - עקרב
Snail - Cheelazonn - חילזון
Invertebrates - Chasrei chool'yot - חסרי חוליות
Shrimps - Chaseelon'eem - חסילונים
Clams - Tzdafoot - צדפות
Crab - Sartan - סרטן
Octopus – Tamnoon - תמנון
Starfish - Kochav yam - כוכב ים
Jellyfish - Medusa - מדוזה

An octopus has eight tentacles.
La tamnoon yesh shmonah zro'ott (tentacles).
לתמנון יש שמונה זרועות.

A jellyfish is a common dish in Asian culture.
Medusa nechshevet le ma'achal (a dish) nafotz ba tarboot (culture) ha asyaty't.
מדוזה נחשבת למאכל נפוץ בתרבות האסייתית.

The museum has a large collection of invertebrate fossils.
La mozei'onn yesh osef (collection) gadol shel chasrei chool'yott meooban'eem (fossils).
למוזיאון יש אוסף גדול של חסרי חוליות מאובנים.

I have crabs and starfish in my aquarium.
Yesh lee sartan'eem ve kochavei yam ba akvar'yoom (aquarium) sheli.
יש לי סרטנים וכוכבי ים באקווריום שלי.

Certain types of spiders and scorpions can be dangerous.
Soog'eem (types) mesooyam'eem (certain) shel akaveesh'eem ve a'krabb'eem yecholeem lehi'yot mesookaneem.
סוגים מסוימים של עכבישים ועקרבים יכולים להיות מסוכנים.

Is there a snail inside the shell?
Ha'eem yesh shablool ba koon'chee'ya (snail shell)?
האם יש שבלול בקונכיה?

RELIGION, CELEBRATIONS, & CUSTOMS
DA'AT, CHAG'EEM, OO MIN'HAG'EEM - דת, חגים ומנהגים

God - Elo'eem אלוהים
God - Elo'keem - אלוקים
Bible – Tanach - תנך
Adam - Adam - אדם
Eve - Chava - חווה
Garden of Eden, heaven - Gan eden - גן עדן
Angels - Mal'ach'eem - מלאכים
Priest (in Judaism) **-** Cohen - כהן
To pray - Lehitpalel- להתפלל
Prayer – Tfeela - תפילה
Blessing - Bracha- ברכה
To bless - Levarech- לברך

What is your religion?
Ma'ee ha dat shelcha?
מה הדת שלך?

Many religions use the bible.
Dat'oot raboot (many) mishtamshot (they use) ba tanach.
דתות רבות משתמשות בתנ"ך.

We have faith in miracles.
Yesh lanoo emoona bae neseem.
יש לנו אמונה בניסים.

Adam and Eve were the first humans and lived in the Garden of Eden.
Adam ve chava hayu bnei ha adam ha rishon'eem ve hem chayoo be gan eden.
אדם וחווה היו בני האדם הראשונים והם היו בגן עדן.

When do I need to say the blessing?
Matai alai lomar et ha bracha?
מתי עליי לומר את הברכה?

I must say a prayer for the holiday.
Ani tzarich/tzreicha lomar tfeela la chag.
אני צריך \ צריכה לומר תפילה לחג.

The angels came from heaven.
Ha malahach'eem heigui'yoo mae hashama'eem.
המלאכים הגיעו מהשמיים.

Holy - Kadosh - קדוש
Faith – Emoona- אמונה
Miracle - Ness - נס
Prophet - Navi - נביא
Moses - Moshe - משה
Messiah - Mashiach - משיח
Noah - No'ach - נוח
Ark - Tei'vah - תיבה
Ten commandments - A'aseret ha dibrot - עשרת הדברות
The five books of Moses - Chameshet sifrei ha torah - חמשת ספרי התורה
Genesis - Beresheet - בראשית
Exodus - Shmot - שמות
Leviticus - Va'ykra - ויקרא
Numbers - Bameed'bar - במדבר
Deuteronomy - Dvareem - דברים

Aaron, the brother of Moses, was the first priest.
A'aron, acheev shel moshe, haya ha cohen ha rishon (first).
אהרון, אחיו של משה, היה הכהן הראשון.
The story of Noah's Ark and the flood is very interesting.
Sipoor (story) teivat noach ve ha mabool (flood) ma'anyen'eem me'od.
סיפור תיבת נוח והמבול מעניינים מאוד.
Moses climbed up on Mount Sinai to receive the Ten Commandments.
Moshe ne'elatz letapes al har seen'ayee kedei lekabel et a'aseret ha dibrot.
משה נאלץ לטפס על הר סיני כדי לקבל את עשרת הדברות.
The Five Books of the Moses are Genesis, Exodus, Leviticus, Numbers, and Deuteronomy.
Chameshet seefrei ha torah; beresheet, shmot, vaykra, bameedbar, ve dvareem.
חמשת ספרי התורה: בראשית, שמות, ויקרא, במדבר ודברים.
Moses was considered as the prophet of all prophets.
Moshe nechshav la navi ha nevi'eem.
משה נחשב לנביא הנביאים.
My favorite book of the bible is the Book of Prophets.
Sefer ha tanach ha ahoov alai hoo sefer ha nevi'eem.
ספר התנ"ך האהוב עליי הוא ספר נביאים.

Jew - Yehoodi- יהודי
Judaism – Yahadoot - יהדות
Religious - Dat'ee - דתי
Religious - (f) Dat'ee'ya - דתיה
Monotheism - Emoona bea el echad- אמונה באל אחד
Synagogue - Beit keneset - בית כנסת

The Jews worship at the synagogue.
Ha yehoodim mitpal'el'eem ba veit ha keneset
היהודים מתפללים בבית הכנסת.

The Bible is a holy book which tells the story of the Jewish nation and includes many miracles.
Ha tanach hoo sefer kadosh shae mesaper et ha sipur shel ha a'am (nation) ha yehoodi ve kolel niseem rabeem.
התנ"ך הוא ספר קדוש שמספר את הסיפור של העם היהודי וכולל ניסים רבים.

The three forefathers are Abraham, Isaac, and Jacob.
Sholoshet ha avot hem avraham, itzack, ve ya'akov.
שלושת האבות הם אברהם, יצחק ויעקב.

The bible is divided into 54 portions according to the 54 weeks to be read in the synagogue.
Ha tanach mechoolak le 54 parashot alpee (according to) shavoo'ot ha shana, otam yesh likro bae beit ha kneset.
התנ"ך מחולק ל - 54 פרשות על פי שבועות השנה, אותם יש לקרוא בבית הכנסת.

In Judaism, they pray three times a day. Morning prayer, afternoon prayer, and evening prayer.
Ba yahadoot mitpalel'eem shalosh pa'am'eem bei yom. Tfilat shacharit, mincha, ve ma'a'riv.
ביהדות מתפללים שלוש פעמים ביום. תפילת שחרית, מנחה ומעריב.

Where is the goblet of wine for Rosh Hashana?
Eichan gaviya ha yaiin (wine) lei rosh hashana?
היכן גביע היין לראש השנה.

Passover – Pesach - פסח
Circumcision - Brit mila- ברית מילה
Menorah - Chanookee'ya - חנוכה
Dreidle - Sevivon - סביבון
Kosher – Kashroot - כשרות
Kosher - Kasher כשר

I want to fast this year on Yom Kippur.
Ani rotzei/rotza latzoom hashana bae yom kippur.
אני רוֹצֶה\רוֹצָה לצום השנה ביום כיפור.
I have a menorah and a dreidel for Hannukah.
Yesh li chanookee'ya ve sevivon le chanukah.
יש לי חנוכיה וסביבון לחנוכה.
Passover is my favorite holiday.
Pesach ha chag ha ahoov alai.
פסח החג האהוב עליי.
We welcome the Sabbath by lighting candles.
Ano makbileem et pnei ha shabat be hadlakat ner'ott.
אנו מקבלים את פני השבת בהדלקת נרות.
I want to keep kosher.
Ani rotzei/rotza lishmor a'l kashroot.
אני רוֹצֶה\רוֹצָה לשמור על כשרות.
Where is your yarmulke?
Eichan ha kipa shelcha?
היכן הכיפה שלך?
The circumcision is performed on the 8th day after the birth of the child.
Brit ha mila mevootza'at (carried out) ba yom ha shmini le'achar lidato shel ha yeled.
ברית המילה מבוצעת ביום השמיני לאחר לידתו של הילד.
There is a large religious Jewish community in this neighborhood.
Ba shchoona hazoot yesh kehila (community) yehudit dat'eet gdola.
בשכונה הזאת יש קהילה יהודית דתית גדולה.
It's very important to learn about the holocaust & concentration camps.
Chashoov me'od lilmod al ha sho'aa ve al machanot ha reekooz.
חשוב מאוד ללמוד על השואה ועל מחנות הריכוז.

Old Testament - Ha breet ha yeshana - הברית הישנה
New Testament - Ha breet ha chadasha - הברית החדשה
The Christian Religion - Ha da'at ha notzreet - הדת הנוצרית
Christian - Notzree - נוצרי
Church - Knesi'ya - כנסייה
Cathedral – Catedral - קתדרלה
Catholic - Catol'ee - קתולי
Catholic - (f) Catol'eet - קתולית
Christianity - Natzroot - נצרות
Catholicism - Catol'ee'oot - קתוליות
Monastery - Minzar - מנזר
Jesus - Yeshoo - ישו
A cross - Tzlav - צלב
Priest (in Christianity) - Comer - כומר
Holy - Kadosh - קדוש
Holy water - Ma'eem kdosheem - מים קדושים
New Year - Shana chadasha - שנה חדשה

The church is open today.
Hayom ha knesi'ya ptoocha.
היום הכנסייה פתוחה.

The priest read a psalm from the Bible in front of the congregation.
Ha comer kara mizmor (psalm) mei ha tanach mool (in front of) ha kehila.
הכומר קרא מזמור מהתנ"ך מול הקבילה.

I went to pray in the cathedral.
Alachti lehitpalel ba catedrala.
הלכתי להתפלל בקתדרלה.

The priest baptized the baby in the holy water.
Ha comer taval et ha tinok bae ma'yeem kdoshim.
הכומר טבל את התינוק במים קדושים.

Happy holiday and Happy New Year to all my friends and family.
Chag sameiach ve shana tova le kol ha chaverim sheli ve bnei ha mishpacha.
חג שמח ושנה טובה לכל החברים שלי ובני המשפחה.

Many schools refuse to teach evolution.
Batei sefer rabim mesarvim lelamed et hitpatchoot-ha-enoshoot (evolution).
בתי ספר רבים מסרבים ללמד את האבולוציה

To sin - Lachto - לחטוא
A sin - Chet - חטא
Christmas - Chag hamolad - חג המולד
Christmas eve - Erev chag hamolad - ערב חג המולד
Christmas tree - Etz ha ashoo'ach - עץ אשוח
Merry Christmas - Chag molad same'ach - חג מולד שמח
Easter - Chag ha pascha - חג הפסחא
Saint - Kadosh - קדוש
Saint - (f) Kdosha - קדושה
Nun - Nezira - נזירה
Chapel - Beit tfila - בית תפילה
Islam - Islam - אסלאם
Muslim - Muslemee - מוסלמי
Mosque - Misgad - מסגד
Hindu - Hindi - הינדי
Buddhist - Bood'eest - בודהיסט
Temple - Mikdash - מקדש

Christians love to celebrate Christmas.
Ha notzreem ohaveem lachagog et chag ha molad.
הנוצרים אוהבים לחגוג את חג המולד.

Is it possible to turn on the lights on my Christmas tree for Christmas Eve?
Efshar (is it possible) lehadlik et ha orot al etz ha shoo'ach sheli le erev chag ha molad?
אפשר להדליק את האורות על עץ האשוח שלי לערב חג המולד?

Two more weeks until Easter.
Rak od shvo'aim (two weeks) a'd chag ha psacha.
רק עוד שבועיים עד חג הפסחא.

The nuns live in the monastery.
Ha nezir'ott gar'ott ba minzar.
הנזירות גרות במנזר.

בתי ספר רבים מסרבים ללמד את התפתחות האנושות.

The Muslims pray at the mosque.
Ha moslemeem mitpaleleem ba misgad.
המוסלמים מתפללים במסגד.

In Islam they pray five times a day.
Ba islam mitpalel'eem chamesh pehameem ba yom.
באסלאם מתפללים חמש פעמים ביום.

WEDDING AND RELATIONSHIP
NESOO'EEM VE ITYACHASOOT - נישואים והתיחסות

Wedding - Chatoona חתונה / **Wedding -** nesoo'eem - נישואים
Wedding hall - Oo'lam chatoonot - אולם חתונות
Married - Nasoo'yee - נשוי
Civil wedding - Chatoona ezrach'eet - חתונה אזרחית
Bride - Kala - כלה / **Groom -** Chatan - חתן
Husband - Ba'al - בעל / **Wife -** Eesha - אישה
Ceremony - Tekes - טקס
Reception hall - Oolam ha kabala - אולם הקבלה
Chapel - Beit keneset - בית כנסת
Engagement – Eerooseem - אירוסים
Engagement ring - Taba'at erooseem - טבעת אירוסים
Wedding ring - Taba'at neesoo'eem - טבעת נישואים

When is the wedding?
Matai ha chatoona?
מתי החתונה?
We are having the service in the chapel and the reception in the wedding hall.
Anachnu nitpalel bebeit ha kneset ve kabalat ha pan'eem tee'hyae bae oolam ha chatoonot.
אנחנו נתפלל בבית הכנסת וקבלת הפנים תהיה באולם החתונות.
Three civil weddings are taking place at the courthouse today.
Shalosh chatoonot ezrachee'yot (civil) mitrachshot (taking place) hayom ba veit ha mishpat.
שלוש חתונות אזרחיות מתרחשות היום בבית משפט.
The bride and groom received many presents.
Ha chatan ve ha kala kibloo harbei matan'ot (presents).
החתן והכלה קיבלו הרבה מתנות.
This is my engagement ring and this is my wedding ring.
Zot taba'at ha erooseem sheli vzot tabat ha neesooyeem.
זאת טבעת האירוסים שלי וזאת טבעת הנישואים.
They are finally married so now it's time for the honeymoon.
Sof sof (finally) hem nesoo'eem az achshav egui'a-ha-zman (the time has come) la ye'rach ha dvash.
סוף סוף הם נשואים אז עכשיו הגיע הזמן לירח הדבש.

Anniversary - Yom ha neesoo'yeem - יום הנישואים
Honeymoon - Ye'rach dvash - ירח דבש
Fiancé - Aroos - ארוס / **Fiancé** - (f) aroosa - ארוסה
Valentine day - Yom ha ahava - יום האהבה
Love - Ahava - אהבה
To love - Le'eh'hov - לאהוב
In love - Mae'o'hav - מאוהב / **In love** - (f) Mae'o'hevet - מאוהבת

I am in love with her (male to female).
Ani mae'hoo'hav ba.
אני מאוהב בה.

I am in love with him (female to male).
Ani mei'hoo'hevet bo.
אני מאוהבת בו.

I love her (male to female).
Ani ohev ota.
אני אוהב אותה.

I love him (female to male).
Ani ohevet oto.
אני אוהבת אותו.

I love you (male to female).
Ani ohev otach.
אני אוהב אותך.

I love you (female to male).
Ani ohevet otcha.
אני אוהבת אותך.

Our anniversary is on Valentine's Day.
Yom ha neesooyeen shelanu be yom ha ahava.
יום הנישואים שלנו ביום האהבה.

He decided to propose to his girlfriend. She said "yes" and now they are engaged.
Hoo hechelit lehatziya neesooeem la chavera shelo. Hee amra "ken" ve achshav hem mehooras'eem.
הוא החליט להציע נישואים לחברה שלו. היא אמרה "כן" ועכשיו הם מאורסים.

He is my fiancé now. Next year he will be my husband.
Hoo ha aroos sheli achshav ve bashana haba'a hoo hee'ee'yae ha bahal sheli.
הוא הארוס שלי עכשיו ובשנה הבאה הוא יהיה הבעל שלי.

Boyfriend - Chaver - חבר
Girlfriend - Chavera - חברה
To hug - Lechabek - לחבק
A hug - Chibook - חיבוק
To kiss - Lenashek - לנשק
A kiss - Neshika - נשיקה
Single - Ravak - רווק
Single - (f) ravaka - רווקה
Divorced - Garoosh - גרוש
Divorced - (f) Groosha - גרושה
Widow - Alman - אלמן
Widow - (f) Almana - אלמנה
Romantic - Romanti - רומנטי
Darling - Yakiri - יקירי
A date - Pgeesha - פגישה
A (non-romantic) **relationship** - Yachaseem - יחסים
A (married relationship) **relationship** - Zoog'ee'oot - זוגיות

You are very romantic.
Ata me'od romanti.
אתה מאוד רומנטי.
They have a very good relationship.
Yesh la'hem yachaseem tov'eem.
יש להם יחסים טובים.
I am single because I divorced my wife.
Ani ravak kee hitgarash'tee mae ishtee.
אני רווק כי התגרשתי מאשתי.
She is my darling and my love.
Hee yakeera'tee ve ahoova'tee
היא יקירתי ואהובתי.
I want to kiss you and hug you in this picture.
Ani rotzei/rotza lenashek ve lechabek otcha/otach ba tmoona (picture) ha zot.
אני רוֹצָה\רוֹצָה לנשק ולחבק אוֹתְךָ\אוֹתָךְ בתמונה הזאת.
The husband and wife are happily married.
Ha ba'al ve ha isha hem mehooshar'eem (happy) bae nesoo'eem.
הבעל והאישה הם מאושרים בנישואים.

POLITICS - MEDENI'YOOT - מדיניות

Flag - Deg'el - דגל
National anthem - Himnon le'oomi - המנון לאומי
Nation - A'am - עם
Nation - o'oma - אומה
National - Le'oomi - לאומי
International - Bein le'oomi - בינלאומי
Local - Mekomi - מקומי
Patriot - Patriot - פטריוט
Patriot - Ohev molad'eto - אוהב מולדתו
Symbol - Semel - סמל
Peace - Shalom - שלום
Treaty - Heskem - הסכם
Treaty - Breet - ברית
Sanctions - Eetzoom'eem - עיצומים

He is a patriot of the nation.
Hoo ohev et ha a'am.
הוא אוהב את העם.

Most countries have a national anthem.
Le rov ha medinot yesh himnon le'oomi.
לרוב המדינות יש המנון לאומי.

This is a political movement which is supported by the majority.
Zot tnoo'a polit'eet shae nit'mechet al yade'ee ha rov.
זאת תנועה פוליטית שנתממכת על ידי הרוב.

This flag is the national symbol of the country.
Ha deg'el ha ze hoo ha semel ha le'oomi shel ha eretz.
הדגל הזה הוא הסמל הלאומי של הארץ.

This is all politics.
Kol ze medeni'yoot polit'eet.
כל זה מדיניות פוליטית

They must impose sanctions against that country.
Alei'hem lahateel eetzoom'eem neg'ed ha medina hazot.
עליהם להטיל עצומים נגד המדינה הזאת.

State - Medina - מדינה
Country - Eretz - ארץ
Country - medina - מדינה
County - Machoz - מחוז
Century - Mei'a - מאה
Majority - Rov - רוב
Local - Mekomi - מקומי
Campaign - Ma'aracha - מערכה
Annexation - Seep'uuach - סיפוח
Plan - Tochn'eet - תוכנית
Strategic - Estrateg'eet - איסטרטגית
Decision - Hachlata - החלטה
Ambassador – Shagreer - שגריר
Embassy - Shagreer'oot - שגרירות
Consulate - Consool'ya - קונסוליה

This is a political campaign to demand independence.
Zot ma'aracha medeen'eet shae doreshet atzma'oot.
זאת מערכה מדינית שדורשת עצמאות.

The annexation plan was a strategic decision.
Toch'neet ha seep'uuach hayta hachlata estrateg'eet.
תוכנית הסיפוח הייתה החלטה אסטרטגית.

There is a difference between state law and local law.
Yesh evdel bein chok ha medina la chok ha mekomi.
יש הבדל בין חוק המדינה לחוק המקומי.

The ambassador's residence is located near the embassy.
Mekom ha megoor'eem shel ha shagreer hoo samooch (near) la shagreer'oot.
מקום המגורים של השגריר הוא סמוך לשגרירות.

I need the phone number and address of the consulate.
Ani tzarich/tzreicha et mispar ha telefon ve ha ktovet (address) shel ha consool'ya.
אני צריך\צריכה את מספר הטלפון והכתובת של הקונסוליה.

Are consular services available today?
Hayeem-nitan (is it possible) lahaseeg she'root'aei (services) ha consul'ee'ya hayom?
האם ניתן להשיג שירותי הקונסוליה היום?

Legal - Chook'ee - חוקי
Law – Chok - חוק
Illegal - Lo chook'ee - לא חוקי
International law - Chok bein le'oomi - חוק בינלאומי
Human rights - Zchoo'yot ha adam - זכויות האדם
Punishment – Onesh - עונש
Torture - Ee'noo'y - עינוי
Execution (to kill) **-** Hotza'at la oreg - הוצאה להורג
Spy - Meragel - מרגל
Amnesty – Chaneena - חנינה
Political asylum - Miklat medeenee - מקלט מדיני
Republic – República - רפובליקה
Election - Becheerot - בחירות
Poll - Kalpee / kalfee - קלפי
Election campaign - Maharachat bechirot - מערכת בחירות
Candidate - Mo'oomad - מועמד

There were many protests and riots today.
Hayoo arbei mecha'ott ve mehoom'ott hayom.
היו הרבה מחאות ומהומות היום.

The civilian population wanted a revolution.
Ha oochloosiya ha ezracheet ratzta mahapaecha.
האוכלוסיה האזרחית רצתה מהפכה.

The politicians want to ask the president to give the captured spy amnesty.
Ha politika'eem rotzeem levakesh mei ha nassee latet chaneena la meragel shae nilkad.
הפוליטיקאים רוצים לבקש מהנשיא לתת חנינה למרגל שנלכד.

In which county is this legal?
Bei ezei machoz ze chook'ee?
באיזה מחוז זה חוקי?

I want to go to the election polls to vote for the new candidate.
Ani rotzei/rotza lalechet la kalfee ha bchirot kedey lahatzbeeya la mo'oomad ha chadash.
אני רוצה\רוצה ללכת לקלפי הבחירות כדי להצביע למועמד החדש.

Dictator - Dictator - דיקטטור
Dictator - Rodan - רודן
Citizen - Ezrach - אזרח
Resident – Toshav - תושב
Immigrant - Mehager - מהגר
Public - Tziboor'ee - ציבורי
Private - Prat'ee - פרטי
Government - Memshala - ממשלה
Revolution - Mahapaecha - מהפכה
Civilian - Ezrachi - אזרחי
A civilian - Ezrach - אזרח
Population - Och'loo'siya - אוכלוסיה
Socialism – Socializm - סוציאליזם
Communism - Comunizm - קומוניזם
Racism - Gaz'an'oot - גזענות
Fascism - Fash'ism - פשיזם

Although he was the brutal dictator of the republic, in private he was a nice person.
Afiloo shae hoo haya rodan achzar'ee (brutal) shel ha republica, bae cha'yav ha prati'eem (private) hay adam nechmad (nice).
אפילו שם הוא היה רודן אכזרי של הרפובליקה, בחייו הפרטיים היה אדם נחמד.

In some countries torture and execution is a common form of legitimate punishment.
Bemedinot mesooyamot eenoo'eem ve hotza'a la'horeg hem onash'eem choo'kee'yeem.
במדינות מסויימות עינויים והוצאה להורג הם עונשים חוקיים.

This is a violation of human rights and international law.
Zo hafara (violation) shel zchoo'yot ha adam ve ha chok ha bein le'oomi.
זו הפרה של זכויות האדם והחוק הבינלאומי.

Communism and socialism were popular in the 19th century.
Comunizm ve tzocializm hayoo mei'koobaleem ba meiha (century) tsha'esrae'ee.
קומוניזם וסוציאליזם היו מקובלים במאה ה - 19.

We support democracy and are against fascism and racism.
Ano tomch'eem (support) ba democratya ve nege'd fash'ism ve gazan'oot.
אנו תומכים בדמוקרטיה ונגד פשיזם וגזענות.

President - Nass'ee - נשיא
Statement - Hatzhara - הצהרה
Presidential - Ness'ee'oot - נשיאות
Vice president - Sgan ha nasee - סגן הנשיא
Defense minister - Sarr ha haganah - שר ההגנה
Interior minister - Sarr ha pneem - שר הפנים
Exterior minister - Sarr ha chootz - שר החוץ
Prime minister - Rosh memshala - ראש הממשלה
Democracy - Democrat'ya - דמוקרטיה
Democracy - Shilton a'am - שלטון העם
Movement - Tnoo'a - תנועה
Politician - Politika'ee - פוליטיקאי
Politics - Política - פוליטיקה
To vote - Lahatzbeeya - להצביע
Majority - Rov - רוב
Independence - Atzma'oot - עצמאות
Party - Meeflaga - מפלגה
Veto - Veeto - וטו
Impeachment - Hadacha - הדחה
Convoy - Shayara - שיירה

They want to appoint him as defense minister.
Em rotzeem lemanot oto ke sarr ha haganah.
הם רוצים למנות אותו כשר ההגנה.
Both parties want to veto the impeachment inquiry.
Shtey ha miflagot rotz'ott lehateel veto al chakeerat ha hadacha.
שתי המפלגות רוצות להטיל וטו על חקירת ההדחה.
I want to see the presidential convoy.
Ani rotzei/rotza lir'ott et shayeret ha ness'ee'oot.
אני רוצֶה\רוֹצָה לראות את שיירת הנשיאות.
In some countries other than the United States, they have a prime minister, interior minister, and exterior minister.
Bemedeenot mesooyamot milvad artzot ha brit, yesh rosh memshala, sarr ha pneem, va sarr ha chootz.
במדינות מסוימות מלבד ארצות ברית, יש ראש ממשלה, שר הפנים ושר החוץ.
I want to meet the president and the vice president.
Ani rotzei lifgosh et ha nassee ve et sgan ha nassee.
אני רוצה לפגוש את הנשיא ואת סגן הנשיא.

United Nations - Ha oom - האו"ם
Condemnation - Gui'noo'ee - גינוי
United States - Artzot ha brit - ארצות הברית
European Union - Ha eechood erop'ee - האיחוד האירופאי
Military coup - Maka tzva'iit - מכה צבאית
Treason – Bgeeda - בגידה
Resistance - Heetnagdoot - התנגדות
Members - Chaverei - חברי
Captured - Tafoos - תפוס
To capture - Leetfoss - לתפוס
Biased - Meshoo'chad - משוחד
Resolution - Hachlata - החלטה
Unilateral - Chad tzdadi - חד צדדי
Bilateral - Du tzdadi - דו צדדי
Rebels - Mordeem - מורדים

All the members of the resistance were accused of treason and had to ask for political asylum.
Kol chavrei ha heetnagdoot shae hoo'shamoo bebgeeda ne'eltzoo levakesh miklat medinee.
כל חברי ההתנגדות שהואשמו בבגידה נאלצו לבקש מקלט מדיני.

This was an official condemnation.
Ze haya guinooee reshm'ee (official).
זה היה גינוי רשמי.

The United Nations is located in New York.
Binyanei-ha (the building of the) oom nimtza'eem bae new york.
בנייני האומה נמצאים בניו-יורק

I am a United States citizen and a resident of the European Union.
Ani ezrach artzot ha brit ve toshav ha eechood ha eerop'ae'ee.
אני אזרח ארצות הברית ותושב האיחוד האירופאי.

The international peace treaty needs to include both sides.
Heskem ha shalom ha bein le'oomi tzarich lichlol et shnei ha tzdadim (sides).
הסכם השלום הבינלאומי צריך לכלול את שני הצדדים.

According to the government, the rebels carried out an illegal military coup.
Lef'ee-ha (according to the) memshala, ha mordeem bitz'hoo (carried out) makat tzva'itt lo chookeet.
לפני הממשלה, המורדים ביצעו מכה צבאית לא חוקית.

MILITARY - TZAVA - צבא

Military / army - Tza'va - צבא
War - Milchama - מלחמה
Combat - Krav קרב
Armed forces - Kochot chamoosheem- כוחות חמושים
Navy - Cheil ha yam - חיל הים
Soldier – Chayal - חייל
A force - Koach - כוח
Ground forces - Koach raglee - כוח רגלי
Base - Bass'ees - בסיס
Headquarter - Mifkada - מפקדה
Headquarter - Mataei - מטה
Intelligence - Modee'een - מודיעין
Ranks - Dargot - דרגות
Sergeant - Samal - סמל
Lieutenant - Sgan - סגן
The general - Aloof - אלוף
Commander - Mefaked - מפקד
Colonel - Aloof mishnei - אלוף משנה
Chief of Staff – Ramatkal - רמטכ"ל

I want to enlist in the military.
Ani rotzei/rotza lehitgayes la tza'va.
אני רוצֶה\רוצָה להתגייס לצבא.

This base is designated for military aircraft only.
Ha bass'ees hazei mae'yoo'ad (designated) le matos'eem tzva'ee'ym bilvad.
הבסיס הזה מיועד למטוסים צבאיים בלבד.

That is the headquarters of the enemy.
Zot mifked'et ha o'yev.
זאת מפקדת האויב.

The chief of staff was the target of a failed assassination attempt.
Ha ramatkal haya ha ya'ad le neesayon eetnakshoot (assassination) koshel (failed).
הרמטכ"ל היה יעד לניסיון התנקשות כושל.

The sniper killed the highest-ranking lieutenant.
Ha tzalaf harag et ha sgan ha bacheer (high ranking).
הצלף הרג את הסגן הבכיר.

Refugee - Pal'eet - פליט
Camp - Machanae - מחנה
Enlistment - Gui'yoos - גיוס
Military draft - Gui'yoos chova גיוס חובה
Reserves - Mee'loo'eem - מילואים
Terrorism - Ter'or - טרור
Terrorist - Mechabel - מחבל
Insurgency - Itkomem'oot - התקוממות
Border crossing - Ma'avar ha gvool - מעבר הגבול
Atomic bomb - Ptzatzat atom - פצצת אטום
Nuclear weapon - Neshek gar'een'ee - נשק גרעיני
Chemical weapon - Neshek cheem'ee - נשק כימי
Biological weapon - Neshek biolog'ee - נשק ביולוגי
Weapon of mass destruction - Neshek le hashmada hamoneet - נשק להשמדה המונית

They need to enlist reserve forces for the war.
Hem tzreicheem legayes kochot meelooyeem la milchama.
הם צריכים לגייס כוחות מילואים למלחמה.
Welcome to the border crossing.
Broochim haba'eem le mahavar ha gvool.
ברוכים הבאים למעבר הגבול.
Military intelligence relies on important sources of information.
Ha modee'een meestamech al mekorot (sources) meida'a (information) chashooveem.
המודיעין מסתמך על מקורות מידע חשובים.
The terrorist group claimed responsibility for the car-bomb attack at the refugee camp.
Kvootzat ha ter'or natla (claimed) achrayoot (responsibility) al peegoo'a mechonit ha tofet ba machanaei ha pleet'eem.
קבוצת הטרור נטלה אחראיות על פיגוע מכונית התופת במחנה הפליטים.
It is impossible to defeat terrorism because it's an ideology.
Ze biltee efsharee lenatzeiach ter'or kee zot ideolog'ya.
זה בלתי אפשרי לנצח טרור כי זאת אידיאולוגיה.
This country has a powerful airforce.
Yesh la medina ha zot cheil aveer chazak (strong).
יש למדינה הזאת חייל אוויר חזק.

Air strike - Hatkafa aveer'eet - התקפה אווירית
Air force - Cheil aveer - חייל אוויר
Fighter jet - Matos krav - מטוס קרב
Military aircraft - Matos tzva'ee - מטוס צבאי
Drone - Mazlat - מזל"ט
Stealth technology - Technolog'ya chamkan'eet - טכנולוגיה חמקנית
Tank - Tank - טנק
Submarine - Tzolelet - צוללת
Weapon – Neshek - נשק
Grenade - Rimon - רימון
Mine - Mokesh - מוקש
Bomb - Ptzatza - פצצה
Sniper - Tzalaf - צלף
Gun - Ekdach - אקדח
Rifle - Rovei - רובה
Bullet - Kadoor - כדור
Missile - Teel - טיל
Missile - Raketa - רקטה
Mortar – Patzmar - פצמ"ר
Cannon - Totach - תותח

The M-16 is a US-made rifle.
Ha M-shesh'esrei hoo rovei mi totzeret (made in) artzot ha brit.\
ה M-16 הוא רובה מתוצרת ארצות הברית.
At the terrorist safe-house, guns, bullets, and grenades were found.
Bebeit hamachbo shel ha mechabl'eem neemtze'oo ekdacheem, kadooreem, ve rimoneem.
בבית המחבוא של המחבלים נמצאו אקדחים, כדורים ורימונים.
The tank fired artillery shells.
Ha tank yara pagaz'ae'ee artilerya.
הטנק ירה פגזי ארטילריה.
The navy was able to intercept a missile.
Chel hayam heetzlee'ach leyaret teel.
חיל הים הצליח ליירט טיל.
The coalition forces struck an enemy arms depot.
Kochot ha coalitz'ya pag'oo bemachsan neshek shel ha o'yev.
כוחות הקואליציה פגעו במחסן נשק של האויב.

Explosion - Heet'potzetz'oot - התפוצצות
Anti tank missile - Teel neg'ed tank'eem טיל נגד טנקים
Anti tank missile - Teel noon'tet - טיל נ"ט
Anti aircraft missile - Teel neg'ed matos'eem טיל נגד מטוסים
Anti aircraft missile - teel noon'mem - טיל נ"מ
Shoulder fire missile - Teel katef - טיל כתף
Ammunition - Tachmoshet - תחמושת / **Artillery** - Artillería - ארטילריה
Artillery shell - Pagaz artiller'ee - פגז ארטילרי / **Armor** - Sheer'yon - שריון
Precision missile - Teel medoo'yak - טיל מדויק
Ballistic missile - Teel balistee - טיל בליסטי
Flare system - Ma'arechet ha eetlakchoot - מערכת ההתלקחות
Supply - Haspaka - אספקה / **Storage** - Ichsoon - אחסון

Shoulder-fired missiles are extremely dangerous and are hard to defend against.
Teel'ae'ee katef hem me'od mesookan'eem (dangerous) ve kashei lehitgonen negd'am.
טיל כתף הם מאוד מסוכנים וקשה להתגונן נגדם.

The flare system is meant as a defense against anti-aircraft missiles.
Ma'arechet ha itlakchoot mo'edet (meant for) le haganah neg'ed teel'ae'ee noon'mem.
מערכת ההתלקחות מיועדת להגנה נגד טילי נ"מ.

An intense missile attack was carried out against the supply forces that resulted in many casualties.
Mitkefet teel'eem ha a'aza bootzha'a (carried out) neg'ed kochot ha haspakah shae garma (which resulted in) le neefga'eem (casualties) rabeem.
מתקפת טילים העזה בוצעה נגד כוחות האספקה שגרמה לנפגעים רבים.

The terrorist cell fired ballistic missiles at the nuclear facility site.
Choolyat (cell) ha ter'or yarta teel'eem balist'eem la'atar mitkan (facility) ha gar'een.
חולית הטרור ירתה טילים בליסטיים לאתר מתקן הגרעין.

Atomic bombs and chemical weapons are weapons of mass destruction.
Ptzatz'ott atom ve neshek cheem'ee hem neshek le hashmadah hamoneet.
פצצות אטום ונשק כימי הם נשק להשמדה המונית

A target - Matara מטרה
A target - Ya'ad יעד
To target - Lechaven - לכוון
Military attack - Hatkafa tvaeet - התקפה צבאית
To attack - Lehatkeef - להתקיף
Intense - A'az- עז
To shoot - Lirot - לירות
Open fire - Liftoach bae'esh - לפתוח באש
Fired - Ya'ra - ירה
Assassination - Chisool חיסול
Assassination - Eetnakshoot התנקשות
Assassination - Retzach רצח
Enemy - O'yev - אויב
Reconnaissance - Siyoor - סיור
To infiltrate - Lehistanen - להסתנן
Invasion - Pleesha - פלישה

There is an invasion of ground forces.
Yesh pleesha shel kochot ha yabasha.
יש פלישה של כוחות היבשה.

The soldier wanted to open fire and shoot at the invading forces.
Ha chayal ratza liftoach bae esh ve lirot bae kochot ha polsheem.
החייל רצה לפתוח באש ולירות בכוחות הפולשים.

The bomb attack was considered an act of aggression and an act of war.
Ha pee'goo'a nechshav kee ma'asae tokpanoot ve ma'asae milchama.
הפיגוע נחשב כמעשה תוקפנות ומעשה מלחמה.

The reconnaissance drone infiltrate deep into enemy territory.
Mazlat ha see'yor heetzlee'ach lehistanen la o'omek shetach (territory) ha oyev.
מזל"ט הסיור הצליח להסתנן לעומק שטח האויב.

The airstrike targeted an ammunition storage site.
Ha tkeefa ha avir'eet koovna neg'ed ha atar le'ichsoon ha tachmoshet.
התקיפה האווירית כוונה נגד האתר לאחסון התחמושת.

The mortar attack and exchange of fire caused injuries and deaths on both sides.
Mitkefet ha patzmareem ve cheeloofei ha esh garmoo (lead to) le ptzoo'eem ve mavet beshenei ha tzdadeem.
מתקפת הפצמרים וחילופי האש גרמו לפצועים ומוות בשני הצדדים.

Exchange of fire - Cheelofei esh - חילופי אש
A cease fire - Afsakat esh - הפסקת אש
Withdrawal - Neseega - נסיגה
To win - Lena'tze'ach - לנצח
To surrender - Lehikana'a - להיכנע
Victim - Korban - קורבן
Injured - Pag'oo'a - פגוע
Wounded - Patzoo'a - פצוע
Deaths - Mavet - מוות
Killed - Aroogeem - הרוגים
To kill - Laharog - להרוג
Prisoner of war - Shavooi milchama - שבוי מלחמה
Missing in action - Ne'edar - נעדר
Act of war - Ma'asae milchama - מעשה מלחמה
War crimes - Pishae'ee milchama - פשעי מלחמה
Defense - Haganah - הגנה
Attempt - Neesayon - ניסיון

The ceasefire agreement included the release of prisoners of war.
Heskem hafsakat ha esh kalal shichroor aseer'ae'ee ha milchama.
הסכם הפסקת האש כלל שחרור אסירי מלחמה.
The army made a public statement to announce the withdrawal.
Ha tza'va hetz'heer bae fombee ve ho'odee'aa a'l ha neseega.
הצבא הצהיר בפומבי והודיע על הנסיגה.
There was a huge explosion as a result of the terrorist attack.
Haya pitzootz adir (huge) kee-totza'a (as a result) mi peegoo'a ha mechabl'eem.
היה פיצוץ אדיר כתוצאה מפיגוע המחבלים.
The commander of the insurgency was accused of serious war crimes.
Mefaked ha itkomem'oot ho'osham (accused) bae peeshae'ee milchama chamoor'eem (serious).
מפקד ההתקוממות האושם בפשעי מלחמה חמורים.
Several of the submarine sailors were missing in action.
Kama mae malachei ha tzolelet ne'edroo ba pae'oola (in the mission).
כמה ממלחי הצוללת נעדרו בפעולה.
First, we need to clear the mines.
Kodem-kol (first of all), ano tzrechim lefanot et ha moksheem.
קודם כל, אנו צריכים לפנות את המוקשים.

Conclusion

Hopefully, you have enjoyed this book and will use the knowledge you have learned in various situations in your everyday life. In contrast to other methods of learning foreign languages, the theory in this current usage is that ever-greater topics can be broached so that one's vocabulary can expand. This method relies on the discovery I made of the list of core words from each language. Once these are learned, your conversational learning skills will progress very quickly.

You are now ready to discuss sport and school and office-related topics and this will open up your world to a more satisfying extent. Humans are social creatures and language helps us interact. Indeed, at times, it can keep us alive, such as in war situations. You might find yourself in dangerous situations perhaps as a journalist, military personnel or civilian and you need to be armed with the appropriate vocabulary.

"This is a base for military aircraft only," you may have to tell some people who try to enter a field you are protecting, or know what you are being told when someone says to you, "Welcome to the border crossing." As a journalist on a foreign assignment, you may need to quickly understand what you are being told, such as "The sniper killed the highest-ranking lieutenant." If you are someone negotiating on behalf of the army, you may need to find another lieutenant very quickly. Lives, at times, literally depend on your level of understanding and comprehension.

This unique approach that I first discovered when using this method to learn on my own, will have helped you speak the Hebrew language much quicker than any other way.

Congratulations! Now You Are on Your Own!

If you merely absorb the required three hundred and fifty words in this book, you will then have acquired the basis to become conversational in Hebrew! After memorizing these three hundred and fifty words, this conversational foundational basis that you have just gained will trigger your ability to make improvements in conversational fluency at an amazing speed! However, in order to engage in quick and easy conversational communication, you need a special type of basics, and this book will provide you with just that.

Unlike the foreign language learning systems presently used in schools and universities, along with books and programs that are available on the market today, that focus on *everything* but being conversational, *this* method's sole focus is on becoming conversational in Hebrew as well as any other language. Once you have successfully mastered the required words in this book, there are two techniques that if combined with these essential words, can further enhance your skills and will result in you improving your proficiency tenfold. *However*, these two techniques will only succeed *if* you have completely and successfully absorbed the three hundred and fifty words. *After* you establish the basis for fluent communications by memorizing these words, you can enhance your conversational abilities even more if you use the following two techniques.

The first step is to attend a Hebrew language class that will enable you to sharpen your grammar. You will gain additional vocabulary and learn past and present tenses, and if you apply these skills that you learn in the class, together with the three hundred and fifty words that you have previously memorized, you will be improving your conversational skills tenfold. You will notice that, conversationally, you will succeed at a much higher rate than any of your classmates. A simple second technique is to choose Hebrew subtitles while watching a movie. If you have successfully mastered and grasped these three hundred and fifty words, then the combination of the two—those words along with the subtitles—will aid you considerably in putting all the grammar into perspective, and again, conversationally, you will improve tenfold.

Once you have established a basis of quick and easy conversation in Hebrew with those words that you just attained, every additional word or grammar rule you pick up from there on will be gravy. And these additional words or grammar rules can be combined with the three hundred and fifty words, enriching your conversational abilities even more. Basically, after the research and studies I've conducted with my method over the years, I came to the conclusion that in order to become conversational, you first must learn the words and *then* learn the grammar.

The Hebrew language is compatible with the mirror translation technique. Likewise, with *this* language, you can use this mirror translation technique in order to become conversational, enabling you to communicate even more effortlessly.

Mirror translation is the method of translating a phrase or sentence, word for word from English to Hebrew, by using these imperative words that you have acquired through this program (such as the sentences I used in this book).

NOTE FROM THE AUTHOR

Thank you for your interest in my work. I encourage you to share your overall experience of this book by posting a review. Your review can make a difference! Please feel free to describe how you benefited from my method or provide creative feedback on how I can improve this program. I am constantly seeking ways to enhance the quality of this product, based on personal testimonials and suggestions from individuals like you. In order to post a review, please check with the retailer of this book.

Thanks and best of luck,
Yatir Nitzany

Also by Yatir Nitzany

Conversational Spanish Quick and Easy

Conversational French Quick and Easy

Conversational Italian Quick and Easy

Conversational Portuguese Quick and Easy

Conversational German Quick and Easy

Conversational Dutch Quick and Easy

Conversational Norwegian Quick and Easy

Conversational Danish Quick and Easy

Conversational Russian Quick and Easy

Conversational Ukrainian Quick and Easy

Conversational Bulgarian Quick and Easy

Conversational Polish Quick and Easy

Conversational Hebrew Quick and Easy

Conversational Yiddish Quick and Easy

Conversational Armenian Quick and Easy

Conversational Romanian Quick and Easy

Conversational Swedish Quick and Easy

Conversational Finnish Quick and Easy

Conversational Arabic Quick and Easy

www.ingramcontent.com/pod-product-compliance
Lightning Source LLC
Chambersburg PA
CBHW062033120526
44592CB00036B/1932